Student Research Workshop 2012

Held at the 50th Annual Meeting of the Association for Computational Linguistics 2012 (ACL 2012)

Jeju Island, Korea
9 - 11 July 2012

ISBN: 978-1-62276-594-2

Printed from e-media with permission by:

Curran Associates, Inc.
57 Morehouse Lane
Red Hook, NY 12571

proceedings.com

Some format issues inherent in the e-media version may also appear in this print version.

Printed by Curran Associates, Inc. (2012)

Association for Computational Linguistics
209 N. Eighth Street
Stroudsburg, Pennsylvania 18360

Phone: 1-570-476-8006
Fax: 1-570-476-0860

acl@aclweb.org

Additional copies of this publication are available from:

Curran Associates, Inc.
57 Morehouse Lane
Red Hook, NY 12571 USA
Phone: 845-758-0400
Fax: 845-758-2634
Email: curran@proceedings.com
Web: www.proceedings.com

Introduction

Welcome to the ACL 2012 Student Research Workshop. As was the case last year, this year we have solicited and accepted both Research and Thesis Proposal papers. We accepted 14 out of the 31 submissions that we received from students in a wide variety of countries. Two papers were withdrawn, and 12 will be presented as posters during the main ACL 2012 Poster Session. We have paired senior members of the research community with each student in order to provide feedback and guidance to our student authors.

The overall quality of the submissions was high and we thank our Program Committee for their excellent feedback and reviews. We also thank our Faculty Advisors, Kentaro Inui, Greg Kondrak, and Yang Liu, for their guidance. We were able to provide most students with conference registration and travel stipends thanks to generous support from the U.S. National Science Foundation, the ACL Walker Student Fund, and the Asian Federation of Natural Language Processing. Finally, thank you and congratulations to all of our Student Research Workshop presenters.

Student Co-Chairs

Jackie C. K. Cheung, University of Toronto
Jun Hatori, University of Tokyo
Carlos Henriquez, Technical University of Catalonia
Ann Irvine, Johns Hopkins University

Faculty Advisors

Kentaro Inui, Tohoku University
Greg Kondrak, University of Alberta
Yang Liu, University of Texas at Dallas

Student Program Committee Members:

Shafiq Joty, *University of British Columbia, Canada*
Annie Louis, *University of Pennsylvania, USA*
Courtney Napoles, *Johns Hopkins University, USA*
Jason Naradowsky, *University of Massachusetts at Amherst, USA*
Vahed Qazvinian, *University of Michigan, USA*
Sravana Reddy, *The University of Chicago, USA*
Alan Ritter, *University of Washington, USA*
Nathan Schneider, *Carnegie Mellon University, USA*
Ashish Vaswani, *University of Southern California, USA*
Ainur Yessenalina, *Cornell University, USA*

Non-Student Program Committee Members:

Anabela Barreiro, *INESC-ID, Portugal*
Anja Belz, *University of Brighton, UK*
Steven Bethard, *University of Colorado, USA*
Michael Bloodgood, *University of Maryland, USA*
Giuseppe Carenini, *University of British Columbia, Canada*
Colin Cherry, *National Research Council, Canada*
Marta R. Costa-jussà, *Barcelona Media Research Center, Spain*
Adrià de Gispert, *University of Cambridge, UK*
David Farwell, *Technical University of Catalonia, Spain*
José A. R. Fonollosa, *Technical University of Catalonia, Spain*
Timothy Fowler, *University of Toronto, Canada*
Masato Hagiwara, *Rakuten Institute of Technology, USA*
Maxim Khalilov, *University of Amsterdam, Netherlands*
Alexandre Klementiev, *Saarland University, Germany*
Jonathan May, *SDL Language Weaver, USA*

Yusuke Miyao, *National Institute of Informatics, Japan*
Saif Mohammad, *National Research Council, Canada*
Enric Monte, *Technical University of Catalonia, Spain*
Borja Navarro Colorado, *Universidad de Alicante, Spain*
Daniele Pighin, *Technical University of Catalonia, Spain*
Xian Qian, *University of Texas at Dallas, USA*
Horacio Rodríguez, *Technical University of Catalonia, Spain*
Paolo Rosso, *Technical University of Valencia, Spain*
Kenji Sagae, *University of Southern California, USA*
Helmut Schmid, *University of Stuttgart, Germany*
Lane Schwartz, *Air Force Research Laboratory, USA*
Xu Sun, *Cornell University, USA*
Hiroya Takamura, *Tokyo Institute of Technology, Japan*
Paul Thompson, *Dartmouth College, USA*
Yannick Versley, *Universität Tübingen, Germany*
Theresa Wilson, *Johns Hopkins University, USA*
Yue Zhang, *University of Cambridge, UK*
Geoffrey Zweig, *Microsoft, USA*

Table of Contents

Conference Program

Monday, July 9, 2012, 6:00-8:30pm

A Broad Evaluation of Techniques for Automatic Acquisition of Multiword Expressions
Carlos Ramisch, Vitor De Araujo and Aline Villavicencio

Detecting Power Relations from Written Dialog
Vinodkumar Prabhakaran

Active Learning with Transfer Learning
Chunyong Luo, Yangsheng Ji, Xinyu Dai and Jiajun Chen

Query classification using topic models and support vector machine
Dieu-Thu Le and Raffaella Bernardi

Evaluating Unsupervised Ensembles when applied to Word Sense Induction
Keith Stevens

Topic Extraction based on Prior Knowledge obtained from Target Documents
Kayo Tatsukawa

TopicTiling: A Text Segmentation Algorithm based on LDA
Martin Riedl and Chris Biemann

Domain Adaptation of a Dependency Parser with a Class-Class Selectional Preference Model
Raphael Cohen, Yoav Goldberg and Michael Elhadad

Extracting fine-grained durations for verbs from Twitter
Jennifer Williams

Discourse Structure in Simultaneous Spoken Turkish
Isin Demirsahin

A Generic Framework for Multiword Expressions Treatment: from Acquisition to Applications
Carlos Ramisch

Towards Automatic Construction of Knowledge Bases from Chinese Online Resources
Liwei Chen, Yansong Feng, Yidong Chen, Lei Zou and Dongyan Zhao

A Broad Evaluation of Techniques for Automatic Acquisition of Multiword Expressions

Carlos Ramisch♣, ♠, Vitor De Araujo♣, Aline Villavicencio♣
♣Federal University of Rio Grande do Sul (Brazil)
♠ GETALP — LIG, University of Grenoble (France)
`{ceramisch, vbuaraujo, avillavicencio}@inf.ufrgs.br`

Abstract

Several approaches have been proposed for the automatic acquisition of multiword expressions from corpora. However, there is no agreement about which of them presents the best cost-benefit ratio, as they have been evaluated on distinct datasets and/or languages. To address this issue, we investigate these techniques analysing the following dimensions: expression type (compound nouns, phrasal verbs), language (English, French) and corpus size. Results show that these techniques tend to extract similar candidate lists with high recall ($\sim 80\%$) for nominals and high precision ($\sim 70\%$) for verbals. The use of association measures for candidate filtering is useful but some of them are more onerous and not significantly better than raw counts. We finish with an evaluation of flexibility and an indication of which technique is recommended for each language-type-size context.

1 Introduction

Taking into account multiword expressions (MWEs) is important to confer naturalness to the output of NLP systems. An MT system, for instance, needs to be aware of idiomatic expressions like *raining cats and dogs* to avoid literal translations.[1] Likewise, a parser needs to deal with verb-particle expressions like *take off from Paris* and with light verb constructions like *take a walk along the river* in order to avoid PP-attachment errors.

Even though the last decade has seen considerable research in the automatic acquisition of MWEs, both in theoretical and in computational linguistics, to date there are few NLP applications integrating explicit MWE treatment. This may be partly explained by the complexity of MWEs: as they are heterogeneous and flexible, there is no unique push-button approach to identify all types of MWEs in all languages (Sag et al., 2002). Existing approaches are either generic but present relatively low precision or they require a large amount of language-specific resources to yield good results.

The goal of this paper is to evaluate approaches for the automatic acquisition of MWEs from corpora (§2), examining as parameters of the experimental context the language (English and French), type of target MWE (verbal and nominal) and size of corpus (small, medium, large). We focus on 4 approaches[2] and the experimental setup is presented in §3. In §4 we evaluate the following acquisition dimensions: quality of extracted candidates and of association measures, use of computational resources and flexibility. Thus, this research presents a comparative investigation of available approaches and indicates the best cost-benefit ratio in a given context (language, type, corpus size), pointing out current limitations and suggesting future avenues of research for the field.

2 MWE Acquisition Approaches

Efforts for the evaluation of MWE acquisition approaches usually focus on a single technique or compare the quality of association measures (AMs) used to rank a fixed annotated list of MWEs. For instance, Evert and Krenn (2005) and Seretan (2008) specifically evaluate and analyse the lexical AMs used in MWE extraction on small samples of bigram candidates. Pearce (2002), systematically evaluates a set of techniques for MWE extraction on a small test set of English collocations. Analogously, Pecina (2005) and Ramisch et al. (2008) present extensive comparisons of individual AMs and of their combination for MWE extraction in Czech, German and English. There have also been efforts for the extrinsic evaluation of MWEs for NLP applications such as information retrieval (Xu et al., 2010), word sense disambiguation (Finlayson and Kulkarni, 2011) and MT (Carpuat and Diab, 2010).

One recent initiative aiming at more comparable eval-

[1] The equivalent expressions in French would be *raining ropes*, in German *raining young dogs*, in Portuguese *raining Swiss knives*, etc.

[2] We consider only freely available, downloadable and openly documented tools. Therefore, outside the scope of this work are proprietary tools, terminology and lexicography tools, translation aid tools and published techniques for which no available implementation is provided.

uations of MWE acquisition approaches was in the form of a shared task (Grégoire et al., 2008). However, the present work differs from the shared task in its aims. The latter considered only the ranking of precompiled MWE lists using AMs or linguistic filters at the end of extraction. However, for many languages and domains, no such lists are available. In addition, the evaluation results produced for the shared task may be difficult to generalise, as some of the evaluations prioritized the precision of the techniques without considering the recall or the novelty of the extracted MWEs. To date little has been said about the practical concerns involving MWE acquisition, like computational resources, flexibility or availability. With this work, we hope to help filling this gap by performing a broad evaluation of the *acquisition process as a whole*, considering many different parameters.

We focus on 4 approaches for MWE acquisition from corpora, which follow the general trend in the area of using shallow linguistic (lemmas, POS, stopwords) and/or statistical (counts, AMs) information to distinguishing ordinary sequences (e.g. *yellow dress*, *go to a concert*) from MWEs (e.g. *black box*, *go by a name*). In addition to the brief description below, Section 4.4 underlines the main differences between the approaches.

1. **LocalMaxs**[3] extracts MWEs by generating all possible n-grams from a sentence and then filtering them based on the local maxima of the AM's distribution (Silva and Lopes, 1999). It is based purely on word counts and is completely language independent, but it is not possible to directly integrate linguistic information in order to target a specific type of construction.[4] The evaluation includes both *LocalMaxs Strict* which prioritizes high precision (henceforth `LocMax-S`) and *LocalMaxs Relaxed* which focuses on high recall (henceforth `LocMax-R`). A variation of the original algorithm, SENTA, has been proposed to deal with non-contiguous expressions (da Silva et al., 1999). However, it is computationally costly[5] and there is no freely available implementation.
2. **MWE toolkit**[6] (`mwetk`) is an environment for type and language-independent MWE acquisition, integrating linguistic and frequency information (Ramisch et al., 2010). It generates a targeted list of MWE candidates extracted and filtered according to user-defined criteria like POS sequences and a set of statistical AMs. It is an integrated framework for MWE treatment, providing from corpus preprocessing facilities to the automatic evaluation of the resulting list with respect to a reference. Its input is a corpus annotated with POS, lemmas and dependency syntax, or if these are not available, raw text.
3. **Ngram Statistics Package**[7] (`NSP`) is a traditional approach for the statistical analysis of n-grams in texts (Pedersen et al., 2011). It provides tools for counting n-grams and calculating AMs, where an n-gram is a sequence of n words occurring either contiguously or within a window of w words in a sentence. While most of the measures are only applicable to bigrams, some of them are also extended to trigrams and 4-grams. The set of available AMs includes robust and theoretically sound measures such as log-likelihood and Fischer's exact test. Although there is no direct support to linguistic information such as POS, it is possible to simulate them to some extent using the same workaround as for `LocMax`.
4. **UCS toolkit**[8] provides a large set of sophisticated AMs. It focuses on high accuracy calculations for bigram AMs, but unlike the other approaches, it starts from a list of candidates and their respective frequencies, relying on external tools for corpus preprocessing and candidate extraction. Therefore, questions concerning contiguous n-grams and support of linguistic filters are not dealt with by `UCS`. In our experiments, we will use the list of candidates generated by `mwetk` as input for `UCS`.

	Small	Medium	Large
# sentences	5,000	50,000	500,000
# `en` words	133,859	1,355,482	13,164,654
# `fr` words	145,888	1,483,428	14,584,617

Table 1: Number of sentences and of words of each fragment of the Europarl corpus in `fr` and in `en`.

As the focus of this work is on MWE acquisition (identification and extraction), other tasks related to MWE treatment, namely interpretation, classification and applications (Anastasiou et al., 2009), are not considered in this paper. This is the case, for instance, of approaches for dictionary-based in-context MWE token identification requiring an initial dictionary of valid MWEs, like jMWE (Kulkarni and Finlayson, 2011).

3 Experimental Setup

For comparative purposes, we investigate the acquisition of MWEs in two languages, English (`en`) and French

[3]http://hlt.di.fct.unl.pt/luis/multiwords/index.html

[4]Although this can be simulated by concatenating words and POS tags together in order to form a token.

[5]It is based on the calculation of all possible n-grams in a sentence, which explode in number when going from contiguous to non-contiguous n-grams.

[6]http://mwetoolkit.sourceforge.net

[7]http://search.cpan.org/dist/Text-NSP

[8]http://www.collocations.de/software.html

(fr), analysing nominal and verbal expressions in en and nominal in fr,[9] obtained with the following rules:

- **Nominal expressions** en: a noun preceded by a sequence of one or more nouns or adjectives, e.g. *European Union*, *clock radio*, *clown anemone fish*.
- **Nominal expressions** fr: a noun followed by either an adjective or a prepositional complement (with the prepositions *de*, *à* and *en*) followed by an optionally determined noun, e.g. *algue verte*, *aliénation de bien*, *allergie à la poussière*.
- **Verbal expressions** en: verb-particle constructions formed by a verb (except *be* and *have*) followed by a prepositional particle[10] not further than 5 words after it, e.g. *give up*, *switch the old computer off*.

To test the influence of corpus size on performance, three fragments of the en and fr parts of the Europarl corpus v3[11] were used as test corpora: (**S**)mall, (**M**)edium and (**L**)arge, summarised in Table 1.

The extracted MWEs were automatically evaluated against the following gold standards: WordNet 3, the Cambridge Dictionary of Phrasal Verbs, and the VPC (Baldwin, 2008) and CN (Kim and Baldwin, 2008) datasets [12] for en; the Lexique-Grammaire[13] for fr. The total number of entries is listed below, along with the number of entries occurring at least twice in each corpus (in parentheses), which was the denominator used to calculate recall in § 4.1:

- Nominal expressions en: 59,683 entries (**S**: 122, **M**: 764, **L**: 2,710);
- Nominal expressions fr: 69,118 entries (**S**: 220, **M**: 1,406, **L**: 4,747);
- Verbal expressions en: 1,846 entries (**S**: 699, **M**: 1,846, **L**: 1,846).

4 Evaluation Results

The evaluation of MWE acquisition is an open problem. While classical measures like precision and recall assume that a complete (or at least broad-coverage) gold standard exists, manual annotation of top-*n* candidates and mean average precision (MAP) are labour-intensive even when applied to a small sample, emphasizing precision regardless of the number of acquired *new* expressions. As approaches differ in the way they allow the description of extraction criteria, we evaluate candidate extraction separately from AMs.

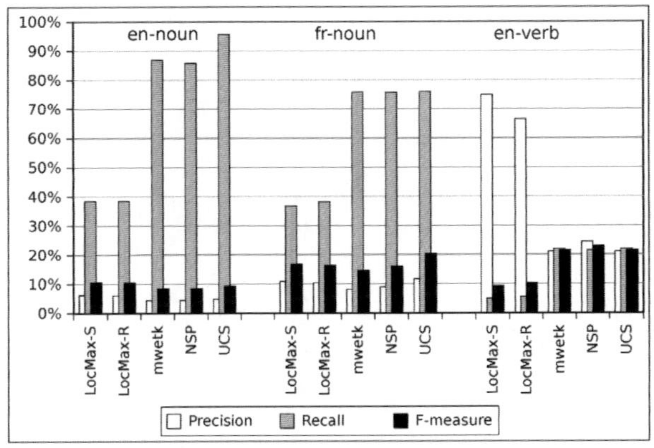

Figure 1: Quality of candidates extracted from medium corpus, comparison across languages/MWE types.

4.1 Extracted Candidates

We consider as *MWE candidates* the initial set of sequences before any AM is applied. Candidate extraction is performed through the application of patterns describing the target MWEs in terms of POS sequences, as described in § 3. To minimise potential cases of noise, candidates occurring only once in the corpus were discarded. We compare the quality of these candidates in terms of (P)recision, (R)ecall and (F)-measure using the gold standard references described in § 3. These measures are underestimations as they assume that candidates not in the gold standard are false MWEs, whereas they may simply be absent due to coverage limitations.

The quality of candidates extracted from the medium-size corpus (M) varies across MWE types/languages, as shown in Figure 1. The candidates for UCS are obtained by keeping only the bigrams in the candidate list returned by the mwetk. For nominal MWEs, the approaches have similar patterns of performance in the two languages, with high recall and low precision yielding an F-measure of around 10 to 15%. The variation between en and fr can be partly explained by the differences in size of the gold standards for each of these languages. Further research would be needed to determine to what degree the characteristics of these languages and the set of extraction patterns influence these results. For verbal expressions, LocMax has high precision (around 70%) but low recall while the other approaches have more balanced P and R values around 20%. This is partly due to the need for simulating POS filters for extraction of verbal MWE candidates with LocMax. The filter consists of keeping only contiguous *n*-grams in which the first and the last words matched verb+particle pattern and removing intervening words.

The techniques differ in terms of extraction strategy: (i) mwetk and NSP allow the definition of linguistic filters while LocMax only allows the application of grep-

[9]As fr does not present many verb-particle constructions and due to the lack of availability of resource for other types of fr verbal expressions (e.g. light verb constructions), only nominal expressions are considered.

[10]*up, off, down, back, away, in, on.*

[11]http://www.statmt.org/europarl/

[12]The latter are available from http://multiword.sf.net/

[13]http://infolingu.univ-mlv.fr/

	S	M	L
		LocMax-S	
P	7.53%	6.18%	4.50%
R	42.62%	38.48%	37.42%
		LocMax-R	
P	7.46%	6.02%	—
R	42.62%	38.48%	—
		P-mwetk	
P	6.50%	4.40%	2.35%
R	83.61%	86.78%	89.23%
		NSP	
P	6.61%	4.46%	2.48%
R	83.61%	85.73%	89.41%
		UCS	
P	6.96%	4.91%	2.77%
R	96.19%	95.65%	96.88%

Table 2: (P)recision and (R)ecall of en nominal candidates, comparison across corpus sizes (S)mall, (M)edium and (L)arge.

like filters after extraction; (ii) there is no preliminary filtering in mwetk and NSP, they simply return all candidates matching a pattern, while LocMax filters the candidates based on the local maxima criterion; (iii) LocMax only extracts contiguous candidates while the others allow discontiguous candidates. The way mwetk and NSP extract discontiguous candidates differs: the former extracts all verbs with particles no further than 5 positions to the right. NSP extracts bigrams in a window of 5 words, and then filters the list keeping only those in which the first word is a verb and that contain a particle. However, the results are similar, with slightly better values for NSP.

The evaluation of en nominal candidates according to corpus size is shown in Table 2.[14] For all approaches, precision decreases when the corpus size increases as more noise is returned, while recall increases for all except LocMax. This may be due to the latter ignoring smaller n-grams when larger candidates containing them become sufficiently frequent, as is the case when the corpus increases. Table 3 shows that the candidates extracted by LocMax are almost completely covered by the candidates extracted by the other approaches. The relaxed version extracts slighly more candidates, but still much less than mwetk, NSP and UCS, which all extract a similar set of candidates. In order to distinguish the performance of the approaches, we need to analyse the AMs they use to rank the candidates.

4.2 Association Measures

Traditionally, to evaluate an AM, the candidates are ranked according to it and a threshold value is applied, below which the candidates are discarded. However, if we average the precision considering all true MWEs as threshold points, we obtain the mean average precision (MAP) of the measure without setting a hard threshold.

[14]It was not possible to evaluate LocMax-R on the large corpus as the provided implementation did not support corpora of this magnitude.

	LocMax-S	LocMax-R	mwetk	NSP	UCS	Total verbs
LocMax-S	—	124	124	122	124	124
LocMax-R	4747	—	156	153	156	156
mwetk	4738	4862	—	1565	1926	1926
NSP	4756	4879	14611	—	1565	1629
UCS	4377	4364	13407	13045	—	1926
Total nouns	4760	4884	15064	14682	13418	

Table 3: Intersection of the candidate lists extracted from medium corpus. Nominal candidates en in bottom left, verbal candidates en in top right.

Table 4 presents the MAP values for the tested AMs[15] applied to the candidates extracted from the large corpus (L), where the larger the value, the better the performance. We used as baseline the assignment of a random score and the use of the raw frequency for the candidates. Except for mwetk:t and mwetk:pmi, all MAP values are significantly different from the two baselines, with a two-tailed t test for difference of means assuming unequal sample sizes and variances (p-value < 0.005).

The LocMax:glue AM performs best for all types of MWEs, suggesting local maxima as a good generic MWE indicator and glue as an efficient AM to generate highly precise results (considering the difficulty of this task). On the other hand this approach returns a small set of candidates and this may be problematic depending on the task (e.g. for building a wide-coverage lexicon). For mwetk, the best overall AM is the Dice coefficient; the other measures are not consistently better than the baseline, or perform better for one MWE type than for the other. The Poisson-Stirling (ps) measure performed quite well, while the other two measures tested for NSP performed below baseline for some cases. Finally, as we expected, the AMs applied by UCS perform all above baseline and, for nominal MWEs, are comparable to the best AM (e.g. Poisson.pv and local.MI). The MAP for verbal expressions varies much for UCS (from 30% to 53%), but none of the measures comes close to the MAP of the glue (87.06%). None of the approaches provides a straightforward method to choose or combine different AMs.

4.3 Computational resources

In the decision of which AM to adopt, factors like the degree of MWE flexibility and computational performance may be taken into account. For instance, the Dice coefficient can be applied to any length of n-gram quite fast

[15]Due to length limitations, we cannot detail the calculation of the evaluated AMs; please refer to the documentation of each approach, cited in § 2, for more details.

	en noun	fr noun	en verb
		Baseline	
random	2.749	6.1072	17.2079
freq	4.7478	8.7946	22.7155
		LocMax-S	
glue	6.9901	12.9383	87.0614
		mwetk	
dice	5.7783	9.5419	46.3609
t-test	5.0907	8.6373	26.4185
pmi	2.7589	2.9173	53.5591
log-lik.	3.166	5.5176	45.8837
		NSP	
pmi	2.9902	7.6782	62.1689
ps	5.3985	12.3791	57.6238
tmi	2.108	4.8928	19.8009
		UCS	
z.score	6.1202	11.7657	46.8707
Poisson.pv	6.5858	12.8226	32.7737
MI	5.1465	9.3363	53.5591
relative.risk	5.0999	9.2919	46.6702
odds.ratio	5.0364	9.2104	50.2201
gmean	6.0101	11.524	45.6089
local.MI	6.4294	12.7779	29.9858

Table 4: Mean average precision of AMs in large corpus.

while more sophisticated measures like Poisson.pv can be applied only to 2-grams and sometimes use much computational resources. Even if one could argue that we can be lenient towards a slow offline extraction process, the extra waiting may not be worth a slight quality improvement. Moreover, memory limitations are an issue if no large computer clusters are available.

In Figure 2, we plotted in log-scale the time in seconds used by each approach to extract nominal and verbal expressions in en, using a dedicated 2.4GHz quad-core Linux machine with 4Gb RAM. For nominal expressions, time increases linearly with the size of the corpus, whereas for verbal expressions it seems to increase faster than the size of the corpus. UCS is the slowest approach for both MWE types while NSP and LocMax-S are the fastest. However, it is important to emphasize that NSP consumed more than 3Gb memory to extract 4- and 5-grams from the large corpus and LocMax-R could not handle the large corpus at all. In theory, all techniques can be applied to arbitrarily large corpora if we used a map-reduce approach (e.g. NSP provides tools to split and join the corpus). However, the goal of this evaluation is to discover the performance of the techniques with no manual optimization. In this sense, mwetk seems to provide an average trade-off between quality and resources used.

4.4 Flexibility

Table 5 summarises the characteristics of the approaches. Among them, UCS does not extract candidates from corpora but takes as input a list of bigrams and their counts.

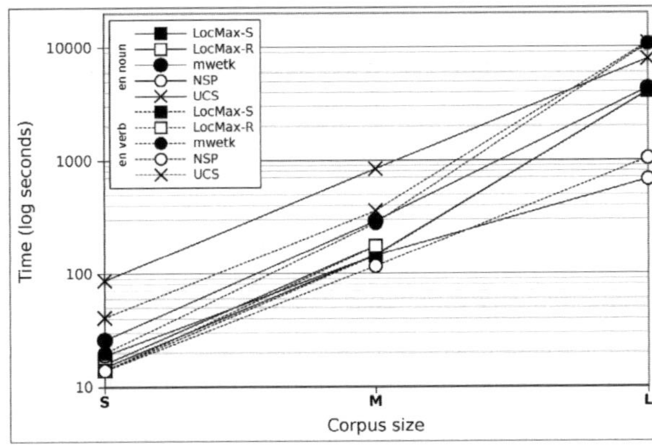

Figure 2: Time (seconds, log scale) to extract en nouns (bold line) and verbs (dashed line) from corpora.

	LocMax	mwetk	NSP	UCS
Candidate extraction	Yes	Yes	Yes	No
N-grams with $n > 2$	Yes	Yes	Yes	No
Discontiguous MWE	No	Yes	Yes	—
Linguistic filter	No	Yes	No	No
Robust AMs	No	No	Yes	Yes
Large corpora	Partly	Yes	Yes	No
Availability	Free	Free	Free	Free

Table 5: Summary of tools for MWE acquisition.

While it only supports n-grams of size 2, NSP implements some of the AMs for 3 and 4-grams and mwetk and LocMax have no constraint on the number of words. LocMax extracts only contiguous MWEs while mwetk allows the extraction of unrestrictedly distant words and NSP allows the specification of a window of maximum w ignored words between each two words of the candidate. Only mwetk integrates linguistic filters on the lemma, POS and syntactic annotation, but this was performed using external tools (sed/grep) for the other approaches with similar results. The AMs implemented by LocMax and mwetk are conceived for any size of n-gram and are thus less statistically sound than the clearly designed measures used by UCS and, to some extent, by NSP (Fisher test). The large corpus used in our experiments was not supported by LocMax-R version, but LocMax-S has a version that deals with large corpora, as well as mwetk and NSP. Finally, all of these approaches are freely available for download and documented on the web.

5 Conclusions and future work

We evaluated the automatic acquisition of MWEs from corpora. The dimensions evaluated were type of construction (for flexibility and contiguity), language and corpus size. We evaluated two steps separately: candidate extraction and filtering with AMs. Candidate lists are very similar, with approaches like mwetk and NSP returning more candidates (they cover most of the nominal MWEs in the corpus) but having lower precision. LocMax-S presented a remarkably high precision for verbal expressions. However, the choice of an AM may not only take into account its MAP but also its flexibility and the computational resources used. Our results suggest that the approaches could be combined using machine learning (Pecina, 2005). The data used in our experiments is available at http://www.inf.ufrgs.br/~ceramisch/?page=downloads/mwecompare.

In the future, we would like to develop this evaluation further by taking into account other characteristics such as the domain and genre of the source corpus. Such evaluation would be useful to guide future research on specialised multiword terminology extraction, determining differences with respect to generic MWE extraction. We would also like to evaluate other MWE-related tasks (e.g. classification, interpretation) and also dictionary-based identification (Kulkarni and Finlayson, 2011) and bilingual MWE acquisition (Carpuat and Diab, 2010). Finally, we believe that an application-based extrinsic evaluation involving manual validation of candidates would ultimately demonstrate the usefulness of current MWE acquisition techniques.

Acknowledgements

This work was partly funded by the CAMELEON project (CAPES–COFECUB 707-11).

References

Dimitra Anastasiou, Chikara Hashimoto, Preslav Nakov, and Su Nam Kim, editors. 2009. *Proc. of the ACL Workshop on MWEs: Identification, Interpretation, Disambiguation, Applications (MWE 2009)*, Suntec, Singapore, Aug. ACL.

Timothy Baldwin. 2008. A resource for evaluating the deep lexical acquisition of english verb-particle constructions. In Grégoire et al. (Grégoire et al., 2008), pages 1–2.

Marine Carpuat and Mona Diab. 2010. Task-based evaluation of multiword expressions: a pilot study in statistical machine translation. In *Proc. of HLT: The 2010 Annual Conf. of the NAACL (NAACL 2003)*, pages 242–245, Los Angeles, California, Jun. ACL.

Joaquim Ferreira da Silva, Gaël Dias, Sylvie Guilloré, and José Gabriel Pereira Lopes. 1999. Using localmaxs algorithm for the extraction of contiguous and non-contiguous multiword lexical units. In *Proceedings of the 9th Portuguese Conference on Artificial Intelligence: Progress in Artificial Intelligence*, EPIA '99, pages 113–132, London, UK. Springer.

Stefan Evert and Brigitte Krenn. 2005. Using small random samples for the manual evaluation of statistical association measures. *Comp. Speech & Lang. Special issue on MWEs*, 19(4):450–466.

Mark Finlayson and Nidhi Kulkarni. 2011. Detecting multiword expressions improves word sense disambiguation. In Kordoni et al. (Kordoni et al., 2011), pages 20–24.

Nicole Grégoire, Stefan Evert, and Brigitte Krenn, editors. 2008. *Proc. of the LREC Workshop Towards a Shared Task for MWEs (MWE 2008)*, Marrakech, Morocco, Jun.

Su Nam Kim and Timothy Baldwin. 2008. Standardised evaluation of english noun compound interpretation. In Grégoire et al. (Grégoire et al., 2008), pages 39–42.

Valia Kordoni, Carlos Ramisch, and Aline Villavicencio, editors. 2011. *Proc.of the ACL Workshop on MWEs: from Parsing and Generation to the Real World (MWE 2011)*, Portland, OR, USA, Jun. ACL.

Nidhi Kulkarni and Mark Finlayson. 2011. jMWE: A java toolkit for detecting multi-word expressions. In Kordoni et al. (Kordoni et al., 2011), pages 122–124.

Éric Laporte, Preslav Nakov, Carlos Ramisch, and Aline Villavicencio, editors. 2010. *Proc.of the COLING Workshop on MWEs: from Theory to Applications (MWE 2010)*, Beijing, China, Aug. ACL.

Darren Pearce. 2002. A comparative evaluation of collocation extraction techniques. In *Proc. of the Third LREC (LREC 2002)*, Las Palmas, Canary Islands, Spain, May. ELRA.

Pavel Pecina. 2005. An extensive empirical study of collocation extraction methods. In *Proc. of the ACL 2005 SRW*, pages 13–18, Ann Arbor, MI, USA, Jun. ACL.

Ted Pedersen, Satanjeev Banerjee, Bridget McInnes, Saiyam Kohli, Mahesh Joshi, and Ying Liu. 2011. The ngram statistics package (text::NSP) : A flexible tool for identifying ngrams, collocations, and word associations. In Kordoni et al. (Kordoni et al., 2011), pages 131–133.

Carlos Ramisch, Paulo Schreiner, Marco Idiart, and Aline Villavicencio. 2008. An evaluation of methods for the extraction of multiword expressions. In Grégoire et al. (Grégoire et al., 2008), pages 50–53.

Carlos Ramisch, Aline Villavicencio, and Christian Boitet. 2010. Multiword expressions in the wild? the mwetoolkit comes in handy. In Yang Liu and Ting Liu, editors, *Proc. of the 23rd COLING (COLING 2010) — Demonstrations*, pages 57–60, Beijing, China, Aug. The Coling 2010 Organizing Committee.

Ivan Sag, Timothy Baldwin, Francis Bond, Ann Copestake, and Dan Flickinger. 2002. Multiword expressions: A pain in the neck for NLP. In *Proc. of the 3rd CICLing (CICLing-2002)*, volume 2276/2010 of *LNCS*, pages 1–15, Mexico City, Mexico, Feb. Springer.

Violeta Seretan. 2008. *Collocation extraction based on syntactic parsing*. Ph.D. thesis, University of Geneva, Geneva, Switzerland.

Joaquim Silva and Gabriel Lopes. 1999. A local maxima method and a fair dispersion normalization for extracting multi-word units from corpora. In *Proceedings of the Sixth Meeting on Mathematics of Language (MOL6)*, pages 369–381, Orlando, FL, USA, Jul.

Ying Xu, Randy Goebel, Christoph Ringlstetter, and Grzegorz Kondrak. 2010. Application of the tightness continuum measure to chinese information retrieval. In Laporte et al. (Laporte et al., 2010), pages 54–62.

Detecting Power Relations from Written Dialog

Vinodkumar Prabhakaran
Department of Computer Science
Columbia University
New York, NY 10027, USA
vinod@cs.columbia.edu

Abstract

In my thesis I propose a data-oriented study on how social power relations between participants manifest in the language and structure of online written dialogs. I propose that there are different types of power relations and they are different in the ways they are expressed and revealed in dialog and across different languages, genres and domains. So far, I have defined four types of power and annotated them in corporate email threads in English and found support that they in fact manifest differently in the threads. Using dialog and language features, I have built a system to predict participants possessing these types of power within email threads. I intend to extend this system to other languages, genres and domains and to improve it's performance using deeper linguistic analysis.

1 Introduction

Social relations like power and influence are difficult concepts to define, but are easily recognizable when expressed. Most classical definitions of power in the sociology literature (e.g. (Bierstedt, 1950; Dahl, 1957)) include "an element indicating that power is the capability of one social actor to overcome resistance in achieving a desired objective or result" (Pfeffer, 1981). Influence closely resembles power, although some consider it as one of the means by which power is used (Handy, 1985). The five bases of power — Coercive, Reward, Legitimate (Positional), Referent, and Expert — proposed by French and Raven (1959) and its extensions are widely used in sociology to study power. I find these definitions and typologies helpful as general background, but not specific enough for a data-oriented study on how they are expressed in online written dialogs.

One of the primary ways power is manifested is the manner in which people participate in dialog. Power relations sometimes constrain how one behaves when engaging in dialog; in some other cases, they enable one to constrain someone else's behavior. And in some cases, the dialog behavior becomes a tool to express and even pursue power. By dialog behavior, I mean the choices one makes while engaging in dialog. It includes choices with respect to the message content, like lexical choices, degree of politeness or instances of overt display of power such as orders or commands. It also includes choices participants make in terms of dialog structure, like the choice of when to participate with how much and what sort of contribution, how many questions to ask and which of those questions to answer and the time between those questions and their answers.

The primary goal of my thesis is to show that different social power relations manifest themselves in written dialog in different, but predictable ways, and to investigate how these manifestations differ across languages, genres and domains. To achieve this goal, I aim to introduce a new typology of power that is relevant in online written interactions and can be validated using data-oriented approaches. Then, I aim to study how these different types of power differ in their manifestations in dialog. Specifically, I aim to capture and compare these manifestations in two dimensions of the dialog: content and structure. In addition to using existing components like dialog act taggers and linkers to capture the dialog structure and lexical analyzers to capture content features, I plan to identify and extract more structural and linguistic indicators of power relations. Using these features, I will build a system that can automatically extract power relations between participants of written dialogs across different languages (English vs. Arabic), genres (discussion forums vs. emails) and domains (political vs. scientific). Currently, I have partially achieved this goal within the context of English corporate email threads, which represent a specific language-genre-domain combination. The four types of power I have defined are: situational power, hierarchical power, control of communication and influence. My future research directions include 1) broadening this work onto other languages, genres and domains and 2) using deeper analysis to identify more indicators of power and capture power relations at finer granularity

2 Literature survey

It has long been established that there is a correlation between dialog behavior of a discourse participant and how influential she is perceived to be by the other discourse participants (Bales et al., 1951; Scherer, 1979; Ng et al., 1995). Specifically, factors such as frequency of contribution, proportion of turns, and number of successful interruptions have been identified as being important indicators of influence. Locher (2004) recognizes "restriction of an interactant's action-environment" (Wartenberg, 1990) as a key element by which exercise of power in interactions can be identified. I use a linguistic indicator *Overt Display of Power* which captures action-restriction at an utterance level. Wartenberg (1990) also makes the important distinction between two notions of power: power-over and power-to. Power-over refers to hierarchical relationships between interactants, while power-to refers to the ability an interactant possesses (may be temporarily) and can use within the interaction. My notions of hierarchical power and situational power roughly correspond to Wartenberg's notions of power-over and power-to, respectively. Both can be considered special cases of French and Raven (1959)'s notion of legitimate power. I consider influence as a type of power which captures notions of expert power and referent power described by French and Raven. Finally, my notion of control of communication is based on the concept of conversational control introduced by Ng and Bradac (1993). It is a form of power the participant has over the interaction; other forms of power are modeled between participants.

In computational literature, several studies have used Social Network Analysis (Diesner and Carley, 2005; Shetty and Adibi, 2005; Creamer et al., 2009) to deduce social relations from online communication. These studies use only meta-data about messages: who sent a message to whom and when. For example, Creamer et al. (2009) find that the response time is an indicator of hierarchical relations; however, they calculate the response time based only on the meta-data, and do not have access to information such as thread structure or message content, which would actually verify that the second email is in fact a response to the first.

Using NLP to analyze the content of messages to deduce power relations from written dialog is a relatively new area which has been studied only recently (Strzalkowski et al., 2010; Bramsen et al., 2011; Peterson et al., 2011). Using knowledge of the organizational structure, Bramsen et al. (2011) create two sets of messages: messages sent from a superior to a subordinate, and *vice versa*. Their task is to determine the direction of power (since all their data, by construction of the corpus, has a power relationship). They approach the task as a text classification problem and build a classifier to determine whether the set of all emails (regardless of thread) between two participants is an instance of up-speak or down-speak. In contrast, I plan to use a complete communication thread as a data unit and capture instances where power is actually manifested. I also plan to study power in a broader sense, looking beyond power attributed by hierarchy to other forms of power. Strzalkowski et al. (2010) are also interested in power in written dialog. However, their work concentrates on lower-level constructs called *Language Uses*, which might indicate higher level social constructs such as leadership and power. This said, one of their language uses is agenda control, which is very close to our notion of conversational control. They model it using notions of topic switching, using mainly complex lexical features. Peterson et al. (2011) focuses on formality in Enron email messages and relates it to social distance and power.

3 Work done so far: Power in Corporate Emails

So far, I have worked on my primary goal – studying manifestations of social power relations – within the context of English corporate email threads. For this purpose, I used a subset of email threads from a version of the Enron email corpus (Yeh and Harnly, 2006) in which messages are organized as threaded conversations. In the remainder of this section, I first introduce the power typology and annotations and then present the linguistic and structural features I used. Then, I present the findings from a statistical significance study conducted between these features and different types of power. Finally, I present a system built using these features to predict participants with power within an email thread.

Power Typology and Annotations: After careful analysis of a part of the email corpus, I defined a power typology to capture different types of power relevant in corporate emails. I propose four types of power: situational power, hierarchical power, control of communication and influence.[1] Person_1 is said to have **situational power (SP)** over person_2 if person_1 has power or authority to direct and/or approve person_2's actions in the current situation or while a particular task is being performed, as can be deduced from the communication in the current thread. Person_1 with situational power may or may not be above person_2 in the organizational hierarchy (or there may be no organizational hierarchy at all). Person_1 is said to have **hierarchical power (HP)** over person_2 if person_1 appears to be above person_2 in the organizational hierarchy, as can be deduced from the communication in the given thread (annotators did not have access to independent information about the organizational hierarchy). Possible clues to HP include (by way of example): 1) characteristic of a part of a message as being an approval, or being a direct order; 2) a person's behavior such as asking for approval; 3) a person's authority to make the final decision. A person is said to have **control of the communication (CNTRL)** if she actively attempts to achieve the intended goals of the communication. These are people who ask questions, request others to take action, etc. and not people who simply respond to questions or perform actions when directed to do so. A thread could have multiple such participants. A person is said to have **influence (INFL)** if she 1) has credibility in the group, 2) persists in attempting to convince others, even if some disagreement occurs, 3) introduces topics/ideas that others pick up on or support, and 4) is a group participant but not necessarily active in the discussion(s) where others support/credit her. In addition, the influencer's ideas or language may be adopted by others and others may explicitly recognize influencer's authority.[2] Prabhakaran et al. (2012a) presents more details on annotations of these power relations in the email corpus.

Manifestations in Content and Stucture: I used six sets of features to explore manifestations of power: dialog act percentages (*DAP*), dialog link counts (*DLC*), positional (*PST*), verbosity (*VRB*), lexical (*LEX*) and overt display of power (*ODP*). The first four sets of features relate to the whole dialog and its structure while the last two relate to the form and content of individual messages. The email corpus I used has been previously annotated with dialog acts and links by other researchers (Hu et al., 2009). I used these annotations to capture *DAP* and *DLC* features. *DAP* captures percentages of each of the dialog act labels (Request Action, Request Information, Inform, Conventional, and Commit) aggregated over all messages sent by the participant within the thread. The dialog links include forward links which denote utterances with requests for information or actions, backward links which denote their responses and secondary forward links which denote utterances without explicit requests that were interpreted as requests and were linked back from later utterances. *DLC* captures various features derived from these links with respect to each participant such as counts of each type of link, counts of forward links that are connected back and counts and percentages of those which were not connected back. *PST* includes features to indicate relative positions of first and last messages by a participant. *VRB* includes features to denote how much and how often a participant took part in the conversation. *PST* and

[1]This typology is an extension of an initial typology formulated through collaborative effort with another student.

[2]I adopt this definition from the IARPA Socio-Cultural Content in Language (SCIL) program, where many researchers participating in the SCIL program contributed to the scope and refinement of the definition of a person with influence.

VRB are readily derivable from the email threads. I used simple word ngram features to capture *LEX*.

Overt display of power (*ODP*) is a linguistic indicator of power I introduced. An utterer can choose linguistic forms in her utterance to signal that she is imposing constraints on the addressee's choice of how to respond, which go beyond those defined by the standard set of dialog acts. For example, if the boss's email is "Please come to my office right now", and the addressee declines, he is clearly not adhering to the constraints the boss has signaled, though he is adhering to the general constraints of cooperative dialog by responding to the request for action. I am interested in these additional constraints imposed on utterances through choices in linguistic form. I define an utterance to have *ODP* if it is interpreted as creating additional constraints on the response beyond those imposed by the general dialog act. An *ODP* can be an order, command, question or even a declarative sentence. The presence of an *ODP* does not presuppose that the utterer actually possess social power: the utterer could be attempting to gain power. In (Prabhakaran et al., 2012b), I present a system to identify utterances with *ODP* using lexical features like word and part of speech ngrams along with dialog acts of the utterance.

Statistical significance study: For each type of power, I considered two populations of people who participated in the dialog – $\mathcal{P}_p$, those judged to have that type of power and $\mathcal{P}_n$, those not judged to have that power. Then, for each feature, I performed a two-sample, two-tailed t-test comparing means of feature values of $\mathcal{P}_p$ and $\mathcal{P}_n$. I found many features which are statistically significant, which suggests that power types are reflected in the email threads. I also found that the significance of features differ considerably from one type of power to another, which suggests that these power types are reflected differently in the threads, and that they are thus indeed different types of power. For hierarchical power, the feature TokenRatio has a mean of 0.38 for $\mathcal{P}_p$ and 0.54 for $\mathcal{P}_n$ with a p-value of 0.07. This suggests that bosses tend to talk less within a thread. People with situational power or control request actions significantly more often than others and send significantly more and longer messages than others. People with influence never request actions and send much longer messages than others. They also tend to have more secondary forward links (with a p-value of 0.07) which suggests that people often respond to what people with influence say even if the influencer's contribution is not a request.

Predicting Persons with Power: I formally defined the problem as: given a communication thread $\mathcal{T}$ and an active participant $\mathcal{X}$, predict whether $\mathcal{X}$ has power of type $\mathcal{P} \in \{\text{SP, HP, INFL, CNTRL}\}$ over some person $\mathcal{Y}$ in the thread. I built a binary SVM classifier for each power type $\mathcal{P}$ predicting whether or not $\mathcal{X}$ has power $\mathcal{P}$ based on features with respect to $\mathcal{X}$ in the context of the given thread $\mathcal{T}$. I obtained good results for SP and CNTRL, but HP and INFL were hard to predict since they occurred rarely in my corpus. The combination of *DLC* and *OSP* performed best for SP (F = 64.4) and *PST* performed best for CNTRL (F = 90.0). For HP, the combination of *DLC* and *LEX* performed best (F = 34.8). For INFL, the best performer was *DLC* (F = 22.6). All results except the ones for INFL were statistically significant improvement over an always-true baseline. I found dialog features to be significant in predicting power, though content features also contribute to detecting some types of power.

4 Proposed Work

So far, I have defined four types of power and have studied how they are expressed and revealed in Enron email threads. My future research directions include deepening this study by i) capturing more linguistic indicators of social power in dialog, ii) building automatic taggers for all linguistic indicators, iii) using deeper semantic analysis on the content and iv) extending it to capture power relations at finer granularity. I also intend to broaden this work into different languages, genres and domains, adapting work done in email threads when viable.

More power indicators : I will work on capturing more linguistic indicators of power from dialog. I currently have annotations at the utterance level that capture attempts to exercise power and attempts to influence. I will use these annotations to build systems that can automatically detect them. In addition, I plan to capture linguistic expressions that suggest lack of power such as asking for approvals, permissions etc. or acting overly polite. For this, I will have to add new annotations to the data. I also plan to perform deeper analysis on the content to capture subjectivity — whether someone states more facts than opinions, commitment — whether someone commits to what she says, and the presence of other modalities such as permissions, requirements, desires etc. I plan to use existing work in subjectivity analysis (Wilson, 2008) and commitment analysis (Prabhakaran et al., 2010) for this purpose. For modality analysis, I plan to use previous unpublished work that I participated in.

Fully automated system: I plan to use automatic taggers to extract dialog act and link features and other linguistic indicators of power (like *ODP*), to build a fully automated social power extraction system. Hu et al. (2009) presented a dialog act tagger and link predictor which could be used to extract *DAP* and *DLC*. However, I found their dialog act tagger performs poorly on minority classes such as requests for actions, which are more critical to predict power. Their link predictor obtained an F measure of 35% which makes it unfit to be used in its current form. For *ODP*, I will use the SVM classifier I built, which obtained a best cross validation F measure of 65.8. I plan to improve the performance of the dialog act tagger, the link predictor and the *ODP* tagger using new features and techniques. I plan to use a threshold adjustment algorithm proposed by Lin et al. (2007) to handle the class imbalance problem in dialog act tagger and link predictor (*ODP* tagger already uses this). I will also build automatic taggers for all other linguistic indicators of power discussed above.

Deeper Semantic Analysis I will explore new features derived from deeper semantic analysis to improve performance of the dialog act tagger, the link predictor and the taggers for other indicators of power like *ODP*. In particular, I plan to use semantic information from VerbNet to provide useful abstraction of verbs into verb classes. This will reduce data sparseness, thereby improving the performance of the taggers. In an initial experiment, I found that using VerbNet class name instead of verb lemma improved the performance of *ODP* tagger by a small margin. I did this only for those verbs that belong to a single VerbNet class (hence needing no disambiguation). I will explore ways to disambiguate verbs with multiple VerbNet class assignments and employ this feature in other taggers as well.

Finer granularity of relations: I will enhance the system to predict power relations between pairs of participants. Aggregating features at the participant level is prone to noise. For example, let $\mathcal{X}$, $\mathcal{Y}$, $\mathcal{Z}$ be active participants such that $\mathcal{X}$ has power over $\mathcal{Y}$, who has power over $\mathcal{Z}$. When we aggregate features with respect to $\mathcal{Y}$, we are introducing noise from the part of communication between $\mathcal{X}$ and $\mathcal{Y}$. Extending my work to the person pair level would prevent this noise and provide us with a finer granularity of power relations. Formally, I want to predict if person $\mathcal{X}$ has power $\mathcal{P}$ over person $\mathcal{Y}$, given a communication thread $\mathcal{T}$. My power annotations already capture the recipient (person_2) of power relations which I will use for this purpose.

Language, genre and domain adaptation: I will extend my work in the English email threads to other languages, genres and domains. Specifically, I plan to work on existing data containing Wikipedia discussion threads and political forums in both English and Arabic. Thus, my thesis would include the analysis of power under 5 different language-genre-domain settings. This step will need extensive annotation efforts. I expect that my proposed power typology might need to be refined to capture types of relations in the new genres. Also, I may have to define new linguistic indicators relevant to the new genres or refine the ones I identified for email threads to adapt to the new genres. This would also require me to adapt various subsystems/taggers to capture features such as dialog acts, links, *ODP* etc. to new genres or build new systems.

5 Conclusion

In my thesis, I propose to study how different power relations are manifested in the structure and language of online written dialogs and build a system to automatically extract power relations from them. I have already conducted this study in English email threads and I plan to extend this to other languages, genres and domains.

6 Acknowledgments

This work is supported, in part, by the Johns Hopkins Human Language Technology Center of Excellence. Any opinions, findings, and conclusions or recommendations expressed in this material are those of the author and do not necessarily reflect the views of the sponsor. I thank my advisors Dr. Owen Rambow and Dr. Mona Diab for their valuable guidance and support. I thank Daniel Bauer for useful discussions and feedback on this proposal.

References

Robert F. Bales, Fred L. Strodtbeck, Theodore M. Mills, and Mary E. Roseborough. 1951. Channels of communication in small groups. *American Sociological Review*, pages 16(4), 461–468.

Robert Bierstedt. 1950. An Analysis of Social Power. *American Sociological Review*.

Philip Bramsen, Martha Escobar-Molano, Ami Patel, and Rafael Alonso. 2011. Extracting social power relationships from natural language. In *ACL*, pages 773–782. The Association for Computer Linguistics.

Germán Creamer, Ryan Rowe, Shlomo Hershkop, and Salvatore J. Stolfo. 2009. Advances in web mining and web usage analysis. chapter Segmentation and Automated Social Hierarchy Detection through Email Network Analysis, pages 40–58. Springer-Verlag, Berlin, Heidelberg.

Robert A. Dahl. 1957. The concept of power. *Syst. Res.*, 2(3):201–215.

Jana Diesner and Kathleen M. Carley. 2005. Exploration of communication networks from the enron email corpus. In *In Proc. of Workshop on Link Analysis, Counterterrorism and Security, SIAM International Conference on Data Mining 2005*, pages 21–23.

John R. French and Bertram Raven. 1959. The Bases of Social Power. In Dorwin Cartwright, editor, *Studies in Social Power*, pages 150–167+. University of Michigan Press.

Charles B. Handy. 1985. *Understanding Organisations*. Institute of Purchasing & Supply.

Jun Hu, Rebecca Passonneau, and Owen Rambow. 2009. Contrasting the interaction structure of an email and a telephone corpus: A machine learning approach to annotation of dialogue function units. In *Proceedings of the SIGDIAL 2009 Conference*, London, UK, September. Association for Computational Linguistics.

Hsuan-Tien Lin, Chih-Jen Lin, and Ruby C. Weng. 2007. A note on platt's probabilistic outputs for support vector machines. *Mach. Learn.*, 68:267–276, October.

Miriam A. Locher. 2004. *Power and politeness in action: disagreements in oral communication*. Language, power, and social process. M. de Gruyter.

Sik Hung. Ng and James J. Bradac. 1993. *Power in language : verbal communication and social influence / Sik Hung Ng, James J. Bradac*. Sage Publications, Newbury Park :.

Sik Hung Ng, Mark Brooke, , and Michael Dunne. 1995. Interruption and influence in discussion groups. *Journal of Language and Social Psychology*, pages 14(4),369–381.

Kelly Peterson, Matt Hohensee, and Fei Xia. 2011. Email formality in the workplace: A case study on the enron corpus. In *Proceedings of the Workshop on Language in Social Media (LSM 2011)*, pages 86–95, Portland, Oregon, June. Association for Computational Linguistics.

Jeffrey Pfeffer. 1981. *Power in organizations*. Pitman, Marshfield, MA.

Vinodkumar Prabhakaran, Owen Rambow, and Mona Diab. 2010. Automatic committed belief tagging. In *Coling 2010: Posters*, pages 1014–1022, Beijing, China, August. Coling 2010 Organizing Committee.

Vinodkumar Prabhakaran, Owen Rambow, and Mona Diab. 2012a. Annotations for power relations on email threads. In *Proceedings of the Eighth conference on International Language Resources and Evaluation (LREC'12)*, Istanbul, Turkey, May. European Language Resources Association (ELRA).

Vinodkumar Prabhakaran, Owen Rambow, and Mona Diab. 2012b. Predicting overt display of power in written dialogs. In *Human Language Technologies: The 2012 Annual Conference of the North American Chapter of the Association for Computational Linguistics*, Montreal, Canada, June. Association for Computational Linguistics.

K. R. Scherer. 1979. Voice and speech correlates of perceived social influence in simulated juries. In *H. Giles and R. St Clair (Eds), Language and social psychology*, pages 88–120. Oxford: Blackwell.

Jitesh Shetty and Jafar Adibi. 2005. Discovering important nodes through graph entropy the case of enron email database. In *Proceedings of the 3rd international workshop on Link discovery*, LinkKDD '05, pages 74–81, New York, NY, USA. ACM.

Tomek Strzalkowski, George Aaron Broadwell, Jennifer Stromer-Galley, Samira Shaikh, Sarah Taylor, and Nick Webb. 2010. Modeling socio-cultural phenomena in discourse. In *Proceedings of the 23rd International Conference on COLING 2010*, Beijing, China, August. Coling 2010 Organizing Committee.

Thomas E. Wartenberg. 1990. *The forms of power: from domination to transformation*. Temple University Press.

Theresa Wilson. 2008. Annotating subjective content in meetings. In *Proceedings of the Language Resources and Evaluation Conference*. LREC-2008, Springer. AMIDA-85.

Jen-yuan Yeh and Aaron Harnly. 2006. Email thread reassembly using similarity matching. In *In Proc. of CEAS*.

Active Learning with Transfer Learning

Chunyong Luo, Yangsheng Ji, Xinyu Dai, Jiajun Chen
State Key Laboratory for Novel Software Technology,
Department of Computer Science and Technology,
Nanjing University, Nanjing, 210046, China
{luocy,jiys,daixy,chenjj}@nlp.nju.edu.cn

Abstract

In sentiment classification, unlabeled user reviews are often free to collect for new products, while sentiment labels are rare. In this case, active learning is often applied to build a high-quality classifier with as small amount of labeled instances as possible. However, when the labeled instances are insufficient, the performance of active learning is limited. In this paper, we aim at enhancing active learning by employing the labeled reviews from a different but related (source) domain. We propose a framework Active Vector Rotation (AVR), which adaptively utilizes the source domain data in the active learning procedure. Thus, AVR gets benefits from source domain when it is helpful, and avoids the negative affects when it is harmful. Extensive experiments on toy data and review texts show our success, compared with other state-of-the-art active learning approaches, as well as approaches with domain adaptation.

1 Introduction

To get a good generalization in traditional supervised learning, we need sufficient labeled instances in training, which are drawn from the same distribution as testing instances. When there are plenty of unlabeled instances but labels are insufficient and expensive to obtain, active learning (Settles, 2009) selects a small set of critical instances from target domain to be labeled, but costs are incurred for each label. On the other hand, transfer learning (Ji et al., 2011), also known as domain adaptation (Blitzer et al., 2006), aims at leveraging instances from other related source domains to construct high-quality models in the target domain. For example, we may employ labeled user reviews of similar products, to predict sentiment labels of new product reviews. When the distributions of source and target domain are similar, transfer learning would work well. But significant distribution divergence might cause negative transfer (Rosenstein et al., 2005).

To further reduce the labeling cost and avoid negative transfer, we propose a framework, namely Active Vector Rotation (AVR), which takes advantage of both active learning and transfer learning techniques. Basically, AVR makes model's parameter vector w actively rotate towards its optimal direction with as few labeled instances in target domain as possible. Specifically, AVR first applies certain unsupervised learning techniques to make source and target domain's distributions more 'similar', and then leverages source domain information to query the most informative instances of target domain. Most importantly, it carefully reweights instances to mitigate the risk of negative transfer. AVR is general enough to incorporate various active learning and transfer learning modules, as well as varied basic learners such as LR and SVM.

2 Related Work

Shi et al. (2008) proposed an approach AcTraK, using labeled source and target domain instances to build a so-called 'transfer classifier' to help label actively selected target domain instances. AcTraK initially requires labeled target domain instances, and relies too much on the transfer classifier. Thus it might be degenerated by negative transfer.

An ALDA framework was proposed in (Saha et al., 2011). ALDA employs source domain classifier w_{src} to help label actively selected target domain instances. When conditional distributions $P(y|x)$ are a bit different (Chattopadhyay et al., 2011) or marginal distributions $P(x)$ are significantly different between source and target domain, ALDA would perform poorly. ALDA doesn't discuss the negative transfer problem and gets hurts when it happens, while AVR actively avoids it by its projection and reweighting strategy.

Liao et al. (2005) proposed a method M-Logit, utilizing auxiliary data to help train LR. They also proposed actively sampling target domain instances using Fisher Information Matrix (Fedorov, 1972; Mackay, 1992). Besides, instance weighting was used to mitigate distribution difference between source and target domain in (Huang et al., 2006; Jiang and Zhai, 2007; Sugiyama et al., 2008). These can work as a module in our framework.

3 AVR: Active Vector Rotation

Without loss of generalization, we will constrain the discussion of AVR to binary classification tasks. But in fact, AVR can also be applied to multi-class classification and regression.

Given training set $D_{tr} = \{(x_i, y_i)|i = 1, \dots, m\}$, $x_i \in R^n$, $y_i \in \{-1, +1\}$, traditional supervised learning tries to optimize (Fan et al., 2008; Lin et al., 2008):

$$\min_w ||w|| + C \sum_{i=1}^{m} \varepsilon(w; x_i, y_i), \quad (1)$$

where the penalty parameter $C > 0$, controls the importance ratio between loss function $\varepsilon(w; x_i, y_i)$ and regularization parameter $||w||$. Loss function's definition is diverse for different basic learners, e.g. LR uses $\log(1 + e^{-y_i w^T x_i})$, while L2-SVM uses $\max(1 - y_i w^T x_i, 0)^2$.

In the paper, we have the following assumptions:

1) Target domain $D_{tgt} = \{(x_u^t, y_u^t)|u = 1, \dots, N_{tgt}\}$, $x_u^t \in R^{n_t}$, $y_u^t \in \{-1, +1\}$, N_{tgt} is the size of D_{tgt};
2) Source domain $D_{src} = \{(x_l^s, y_l^s)|l = 1, \dots, N_{src}\}$, $x_l^s \in R^{n_s}$, $y_l^s \in \{-1, +1\}$, N_{src} is the size of D_{src};
3) $p(x^s) \neq p(x^t)$;
4) N_{src} and N_{tgt} are large enough;
5) Testing set D_{test} and D_{tgt} are i.i.d..

Under maximum labeling budget N_b, our goal is to employ source and target domain instances to maximize model accuracy:

$$\max_w a_{D_{test}}(w) = \sum_{(x_i, y_i) \in D_{test}} \frac{1 + y_i h_w(x_i)}{2 y_i^2}, \quad (2)$$

where the hypothesis is:

$$h_w(x) = \begin{cases} -1, & w^T x < 0 \\ +1, & w^T x \geq 0 \end{cases}. \quad (3)$$

So, we design the machine learning framework, Active Vector Rotation, to optimize w:

$$\min_w ||w|| + \sum_{i=1}^{m} c_i \varepsilon(w; x_i, y_i), \quad (4)$$

where the weight variables $c_i > 0$, control the importance of each instance in training. Larger c_i means more necessity of w to fit (x_i, y_i). Intuitively, w of D_{tr} should try harder to fit the instances from D_{tgt} than the instances from D_{src}, so that the corresponding c_i of instances from D_{tgt} should be larger. The algorithm of AVR is described in Table 1, which is discussed in detail in the following subsections.

Input: D_{src}, D_{tgt}, D_{test}, N_b; Output: w, $a_{D_{test}}(w)$

1. Project x^s and x^t to a common latent semantic space, where $x^{s'}$, $x^{t'} \in R^n$.
2. Actively select the least source domain instances, which can characterize source domain classifier w_{src}, into training set $D_{tr} = \{(x_i^{s'}, y_i^{s'})|i = 1, \dots, N'_{src}\}$.
3. Initialize w using D_{tr}.
4. For $i = N'_{src} + 1 : N'_{src} + N_b$
   1) Actively select the most informative instance $(x_i^{t'}, y_i^{t'})$ from D_{tgt}.
   2) Insert the new labeled instance into training set, $D_{tr} = D_{tr} \cup (x_i^{t'}, y_i^{t'})$.
   3) Update c_j for $j = 1 : i$.
   4) Retrain w using D_{tr} and (4).

   end
5. Compute $a_{D_{test}}(w)$.

Table 1: AVR algorithm

3.1 Projection of Source and Target Domain

x^s and x^t might be in different vector spaces. To employ D_{src} in the training of D_{tgt}'s optimal w, we'd better project x^s and x^t into a common n-dimensional latent semantic space, where the distributions of the projected $x^{s'}$, $x^{t'} \in R^n$ would be more similar. Varied projection approaches could be employed in different tasks. For example, Hardoon et al. (2004) used CCA to project text and image to a latent semantic space, where image could be retrieved by text. Blitzer et al. (2007) and Ji et al. (2011) utilized SCL and VMVPCA respectively in sentiment classification. Huang et al. (2006) applied RKHS and KMM in breast cancer prediction.

Regarding the case where x^s and x^t are in the same vector space but certain approach is applied to make their distributions more similar, we also consider it as a kind of projection of D_{src} and D_{tgt}.

3.2 Initialization of Training set

To reduce training cost and risk of negative transfer, AVR actively selects a relatively small set of instances from D_{src} into D_{tr}. Transfer learning mainly leverages D_{src}'s separating hyperplane information, i.e. w_{src}, while only a small set of critical instances from D_{src} can characterize the statistics of w_{src}. AVR initializes D_{tr} by these critical instances. Different tasks may employ different selection strategy. E.g. in our experiments, the text classification task employs uncertainty sampling (Settles, 2009), while sentiment classification task selects the least N'_{src} instances which can accurately characterize w_{src}, such that:

$$\min_{1\le j_i\le N_{src}} \sum_{i=1}^{N'_{src}} w_{src}^T x_{j_i}^{s'}. \qquad (5)$$

3.3 Query Strategy in Target Domain

After initialization of D_{tr}, AVR uses certain basic learner, such as LR and SVM, to get $w = w_{init}$. As the labeling budget N_b is limited, we need iteratively query the most informative instance and add the new labeled instance into D_{tr} to retrain w.

AVR revises the query strategy of traditional active learning. After a few new labeled instances added to D_{tr}, the retrained w would be different from w_{init} and closer to the optimum. Traditional active learning queries the instance in D_{tgt} w.r.t. w, e.g. uncertainty sampling queries the instance closest to separating hyperplane, such that:

$$\min_{x_i^{t'}\in D_{tgt}} \left|w^T x_i^{t'}\right|. \qquad (6)$$

However, AVR queries the most informative instance from which are identically classified by w and w_{init}, e.g. for uncertainty sampling, AVR queries the instance such that:

$$\min_{x_i^{t'}\in D_{tgt},\ w^T x_i^{t'} w_{init}^T x_i^{t'}>0} \left|w^T x_i^{t'}\right|. \qquad (7)$$

The instance queried by AVR makes w more quickly approach to its optimum, as to some extent, part of the statistics of the instances which are differently classified by w and w_{init}, can be characterized by the new queried instances. But when w is very close to the optimum, AVR will query by traditional active learning strategy.

3.4 Reweighting c_i

Appropriate reweighting can help accelerate w rotating to the optimum and avoid negative transfer. Intuitively, the instances from D_{tgt} and the instances which have similar distribution with D_{tgt} should be given higher weight. Varied reweighting strategy, e.g. TrAdaBoost (Dai et al., 2007), could be applied in AVR framework. In our experiments, AVR employs a simple but efficient reweighting strategy, without iteration:

$$c_i = \begin{cases} 1, i \le N'_{src}, w^T x_i^{s'} w_{init}^T x_i^{s'} > 0 \\ 0, i \le N'_{src}, w^T x_i^{s'} w_{init}^T x_i^{s'} \le 0 \\ b, otherwise. \end{cases} \qquad (8)$$

4 Experiments

We perform AVR on a set of toy data and two real world datasets, 20 Newsgroups Dataset [1] and Multi-Domain Sentiment Dataset[2], comparing it with several baseline methods. In this paper, we use model accuracy $a_{D_{test}}(w)$ under fixed labeling budget N_b as the evaluation. We used LR and L2-SVM as basic learner respectively, but due to space limit, we only report the results of LR.

4.1 Toy Data

We generate four bivariate Gaussian distributions as the positive and negative instances of D_{src} and D_{tgt} respectively as illustrated in Figure 1.

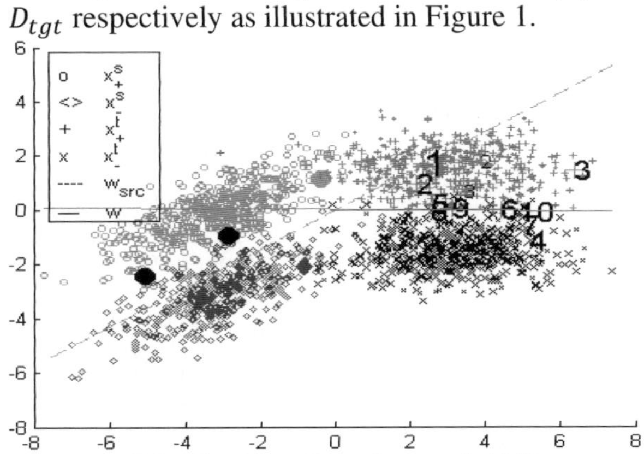

Figure 1: Distribution of toy data and AVR process

[1] http://people.csail.mit.edu/jrennie/20Newsgroups/.
[2] http://www.cs.jhu.edu/~mdredze/datasets/sentiment/.

As shown in Figure 1, D_{src} and D_{tgt} randomly sample 1000 instances respectively, then D_{test} randomly samples 200 instances from D_{tgt}. Circle and diamond, big plus and cross, small plus and cross, represent positive and negative instances of D_{src}, D_{tgt} and D_{test} respectively.

To this toy data, AVR's configuration is:

1) $x^{s'} = x^s, x^{t'} = x^t$.
2) AVR uses uncertainty sampling to select the least 5 instances which can characterize w_{src}, to initialize D_{tr} and w_{init}. In Figure 1, the 5 instances are marked by big filled circles or diamonds, the dash line draws the separating hyperplane $w_{init}^T x = 0$.
3) Then AVR queries instances as described in Section 3.3, the first 10 queried instances are marked by large numerals, with the first 3 are queried w.r.t. (7). The small numerals mark the first 3 instances which would be queried w.r.t. (6).
4) AVR reweights c_i by (8), where $b = 4$. The black filled circles mark the instances whose corresponding $c_i = 0$. The solid line draws the current hyperplane $w^T x = 0$.

Baseline methods are briefly described in Table 2. Details about AcTraK and ALDA can be found in (Shi et al., 2008) and (Saha et al., 2011) respectively.

Method	Note
Random	Randomly sample instances from D_{tgt}, without use of D_{src}
Active	Uncertainty sampling, without use of D_{src}
AcTraK	Initiated by one positive and one negative instances from D_{tgt}, followed by uncertainty sampling from D_{tgt}
O-ALDA	Stream-based sampling, without instance reweighting
B-ALDA	Pool-based sampling, without instance reweighting
Source-A	Initialize D_{tr} by D_{src}, following uncertainty sampling without instance reweighting
AVR-U	Uncertainty sampling with instance reweighting
AVR-W	Give all instances from D_{src} the same weight, regardless prediction difference between w and w_{init}.

Table 2: Brief description of baseline methods

The first 4 methods referring randomness are run 1000 times to average results as shown in Table 3.

Method	Target Domain Labeling Budget N_b									
	1	2	3	4	5	6	7	8	9	10
Random	50.05	69.35	79.88	86.04	90.26	93.01	94.41	95.30	96.03	96.41
Active	49.90	75.65	90.41	95.92	96.30	97.23	97.41	97.59	97.64	97.72
AcTraK	**93.15**	**95.23**	**96.10**	96.69	97.03	**97.30**	97.53	97.68	97.78	97.82
O-ALDA	77	77	77.01	77.07	77.15	77.24	77.33	77.37	77.42	77.48
B-ALDA	77	77	77	77	77	77	77	77.50	77.50	77.50
Source-A	77	77	77	77	77	77	77	77.50	77.50	77.50
AVR-U	80.50	95	85	96	**98.50**	96	98	**98**	97	96.50
AVR-W	80.50	94	94.50	**97**	**98.50**	97	**98.50**	97.50	**98.50**	97
AVR	80.50	94	94.50	**97**	**98.50**	97	**98.50**	97.50	**98.50**	**98.50**

Table 3: Performance of different methods on toy data, where AcTraK unfairly uses two more labels.

4.2 20 Newsgroups Dataset

20 Newsgroups Dataset is commonly used in machine learning and NLP tasks. It contains about 20000 newsgroup documents which are categorized into 6 top categories and 20 subcategories. We split it into 6 pair of D_{src} and D_{tgt}, with each pair includes only two top categories documents, such as "comp" and "rec", but D_{src} and D_{tgt} are drawn from different subcategories, e.g. D_{src} has "comp.graphics" and "comp.graphics", but D_{tgt} has "comp.windows.x" and "sci.autos". The task is to leverage D_{src} to distinguish the top categories of documents in D_{tgt}. Our settings of 20 Newsgroups Dataset is identical with Dai et al. (2007), details can be found there.

On this dataset, AVR's configuration is similar with that on toy data, with N'_{src} varies from 500 to 800 on different pairs.

Due to space limit, we only report results on the pair of "comp vs. rec" in Figure 2, with all methods are averaged over 30 runs. The results on other pairs are similar. Since AVR-U and AVR-W are variants of AVR, with similar performance, we only report the results of AVR.

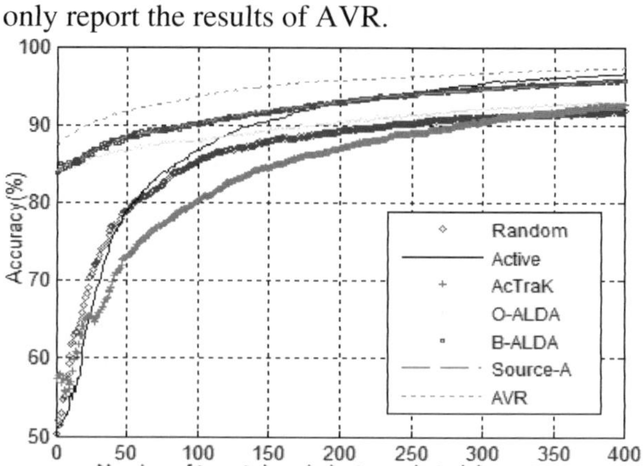

Figure 2: AVR outperforms others on the "comp vs. rec" pair.

4.3 Multi-Domain Sentiment Dataset

The sentiment dataset consists of user reviews about several products (Book, DVD, Electronic, Kitchen) from Amazon.com, the task is to classify a review's sentiment label as positive or negative. We have 12 pairs with each pair has two products as D_{src} and D_{tgt} respectively. On this dataset, AVR employs VMVPCA (Ji et al., 2011) to project D_{src} and D_{tgt}, and initializes D_{tr} with $N'_{src} = 1000$ instances from D_{src} w.r.t. (5), while the other configuration is the same as that described in Section 4.1. To be comparable, the baseline methods which leverage D_{src} are preprocessed by VMVPCA. We also add another baseline method Source-A' here, which is identical with Source-A, except that it is not projected by VMVPCA. Given space limit, we only report the results on the pair "DVD→Kitchen", with other pairs have similar performance.

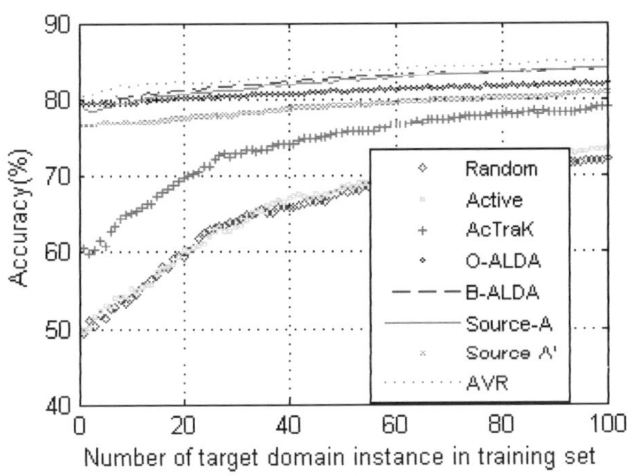

Figure 3: AVR does better than previous work on the "DVD→Kitchen" dataset for all budget sizes.

4.4 Discussion

From inspection of experimental results, we get the following remarks.

Why to combine active learning and transfer learning?

- Active learning such as uncertainty sampling can significantly reduce the labeling cost. But when w is far from the optimum, uncertainty sampling may oversample instances near a direction. For example, in Figure 2, Active method is worse than Random method when $N_b < 50$.
- D_{src} could help D_{tgt} in learning accurate w, e.g. in Figure 2, when $N_b < 200$, Source-A method with the help of D_{src} outperforms Random and Active methods which never use D_{src}. But inappropriate use of D_{src} may cause negative transfer, e.g. in Figure 2, when $N_b > 200$, Source-A, ALDA and AcTraK methods, which overuse D_{src}, underperform Active method.
- Thus, we realize that appropriate combination of transfer learning and active learning could advance and complement each other. Especially when D_{tgt} has scarce labels, D_{src} could help avoid oversample instances near a direction. But with the increase of labels in D_{tgt}, D_{src} should decrease its weight in training to avoid negative transfer.

Does each component of AVR work?

- Appropriate Projection of D_{src} and D_{tgt} could mitigate distribution divergence, e.g. in our sentiment classification task, Source-A and AVR which applied VMVPCA significantly and consistently outperforms Source-A'.
- Initialize D_{tr} by a small set of critical instances from D_{src} can significantly reduce training cost without loss of accuracy. E.g. in our experiments, when $N_b = 1$, AVR has better or comparable performance w.r.t. Source-A which initializes D_{tr} by whole D_{src}. More importantly, AVR trims initial D_{tr} size from 1000 to 5 in toy data, from 4000 to 500 in Newsgroups dataset, and from 2000 to 1000 in Sentiment dataset.
- The query strategy of AVR described in Section 3.3 advances traditional active learning, which is supported by the performance of AVR over AVR-U.
- Appropriately reweighting instances from D_{src} and D_{tgt} could result in accurate w and avoid negative transfer meanwhile. For example, in our experiments, the reweighting strategy of (8) makes AVR outperform all baseline methods, while some of which suffer from negative transfer.

How about AcTraK's performance?

- AcTraK works well on our toy data, just because it unfairly uses too much more labels of D_{tgt}, even though, it underperforms AVR when $N_b > 3$. Besides, AcTraK performs poorly on high dimensional data like text in our experiments.

5 Conclusion and Future Work

Our proposed machine learning framework AVR actively and carefully leverages information of source domain to query the most informative instances in target domain, as well as to train the best possible model of target domain. The four essential components of AVR, which establish its efficacy and help it avoid negative transfer, are validated in experiments.

In the future, we are planning to apply AVR in more tasks with appropriate specification of projection, query and reweighting strategy. Especially for sentiment classification, we will combine prior domain knowledge, such as domain sentiment lexicon, with AVR framework to further reduce labeling cost.

Acknowledgements

This work is supported by the National Fundamental Research Program of China (2010CB327903) and the Doctoral Fund of Ministry of Education of China (20110091110003). We also thank Shujian Huang, Ning Xi, Yinggong Zhao, and anonymous reviewers for their greatly helpful comments.

References

John Biltzer, Ryan Mcdonald, Fernando Pereira. 2006. Domain adaptation with structural correspondence learning. In *Proc.EMNLP*, pp.120-128.

John Biltzer, Mark Dredze, Fernando Pereira. 2007. Biographies, bollywood, boom-boxes and blenders: domain adaptation for sentiment classification. In *Proc. ACL*, pp.432-439.

Rita Chattopadhyay, Jieping Ye, Sethuraman Panchanathan, Wei Fan, Ian Davidson. 2011. Multi-source domain adaptation and its application to early detection of fatigue. In *Proc. KDD*, pp.717-725.

Wenyuan Dai, Qiang Yang, Gui-Rong Xue, Yong Yu. 2007. Boosting for transfer learning. In *Proc. ICML*, pp.93-200.

Rong-En Fan, Kai-Wei Chang, Cho-Jui Hsieh, Xiang-Rui Wang, Chih-Jen Lin. 2008. Liblinear: a library for large linear classification. *JMLR*, 9:1871-1874.

Valeriĭ Vadimovich Fedorov. 1972. Theory of optimal experiments. Academic Press.

David R. Hardoon, Sandor Szedmak, John Shaew-Taylor. 2004. Canonical correlation analysis: An overview with application to learning methods. *Neural Computation*, 16(12): 2639-2664.

Jiayuan Huang, Alexander J. Smola, Arthur Gretton, Karsten M. Borgwardt, Bernhard Schölkpf. 2006. Correcting sample selection bias by unlabeled data. In *Proc. NIPS*, pp.601-608.

Yangsheng Ji, Jiajun Chen, Gang Niu, Lin Shang, Xinyu Dai. 2011. Transfer learning via multi-view principal component analysis. *JCST*, 26(1):81-98.

Jing Jiang, ChengXiang Zhai. 2007. Instance weighting for domain adaptation in NLP. In *proc. ACL*, pp.264-271.

Xuejun Liao, Ya Xue, Lawrence Cain. 2005. Logistic regression with an auxiliary data source. In *Proc. ICML*, pp.505-512.

Chih-Jen Lin, Ruby C. Weng, S. Sathiya Keerthi. 2008. Trust region newton method for large-scale logistic regression. *JMLR*, 9:627-650.

David J. C. Mackay. 1992. Information-based objective functions for active data selection. *Neural Computation*, 5:590-604.

Michael T. Rosenstein, Zvika Marx, Leslie Pack Kaelbling, Thomas G. Dietterich. 2005. To transfer or not to transfer. In *Proc. NIPS*, December 9-10.

Avishek Saha, Piyush Rai, Hal Daumé III, Suresh Venkatasubramanian, Scott L. DuVall. 2011. Active supervised domain adaptation. In *Proc. ECML-PKDD*, pp.97-112.

Burr Settles. 2009. Active learning Literature Survey. In *Computer Sciences Technology Report 1648*, University of Wisconsin-Madison.

Xiaoxiao Shi, Wei Fan, Jiangtao Ren. 2008. Actively transfer domain knowledge. In *Proc. ECML-PKDD* pp.342-357.

Masashi Sugiyama, Shinichi Nakajima, Hisashi Kashima, Paul von Bünau, Motoaki Kawanabe. 2008. Direct importance estimation with model selection and its application to covariate shift adaptation. *NIPS*, pp.1433-1440.

Query classification using topic models and support vector machine

Dieu-Thu Le
University of Trento, Italy
dieuthu.le@disi.unitn.it

Raffaella Bernardi
University of Trento, Italy
bernardi@disi.unitn.it

Abstract

This paper describes a query classification system for a specialized domain. We take as a case study queries asked to a search engine of an art, cultural and history library and classify them against the library cataloguing categories. We show how click-through links, i.e., the links that a user clicks after submitting a query, can be exploited for extracting information useful to enrich the query as well as for creating the training set for a machine learning based classifier. Moreover, we show how Topic Model can be exploited to further enrich the query with hidden topics induced from the library meta-data. The experimental evaluations show that this system considerably outperforms a matching and ranking classification approach, where queries (and categories) were also enriched with similar information.

1 Introduction

Query classification (QC) is the task of automatically labeling user queries into a given target taxonomy. Providing query classification can help the information providers understand users' needs based on the categories that the users are searching for. The main challenges of this task come from the nature of user queries, which are usually very short and ambiguous. Since queries contain only several to a dozen words, a QC system often requires either a rather large training set or an enrichment of queries with other information (Shen et al., 2006a), (Broder et al., 2007).

This study will focus on QC in art, culture and history domain, using the Bridgeman art library[1], although our framework is general enough to be used in different domains. Manually creating a training set of queries to build a classifier in a specific domain is very time-consuming. In this study, we will describe our method of automatically creating a training set based on the click-through links and how we build an SVM (Support Vector Machine) classifier with the integration of enriched information. In (Le et al., 2011), it has been shown that click-through information and topic models are useful for query enrichment when the ultimate goal is query classification. We will follow this enrichment step, but integrate this information into a SVM classifier instead of using matching and ranking between queries and categories as in (Le et al., 2011).

The purpose of this paper is to determine (1) whether the query enrichment with click-though information and hidden topics is useful for a machine learning query classification system using SVM; and (2) whether integrating this enriched information into a machine learning classifier can perform better than the matching and ranking system.

In the next section, we will briefly review the main streams of related work in QC. In section 3, we will describe the Bridgeman art library. Section 4 accounts for our proposed query classification framework. In section 5, we will present our experiment and evaluation. Section 6 concludes by discussing our main achievements and proposing future work.

2 Related work

Initial studies in QC classify queries into several different types based on the information needed by the user. (Broder, 2002) considered three different types of queries: informational queries, navigational queries and transactional queries. This stream of study focuses on the type of the queries, rather than topical classification of the queries.

Another stream of work deals with the problem

[1] http://www.bridgemanart.com/

of classifying queries into a more complex taxonomy containing different topics. Our study falls into this second stream. To classify queries considering their meaning, some work considered only information available in queries (e.g., (Beitzel et al., 2005) only used terms in queries). Some other work has attempted to enrich queries with information from external online dataset, e.g., web pages (Shen et al., 2006a; Broder et al., 2007) and web directories (Shen et al., 2006b). Our work is similar to their in the idea of exploiting additional dataset. However, instead of using search engines as a way of collecting relevant documents, we use the metadata of the library itself as a reference set. Furthermore, we employ topic models to analyze topics for queries, rather than enriching queries with words selected from those webpages directly as in (Shen et al., 2006a; Broder et al., 2007).

The context of a given query can provide useful information to determine its categories. Previous studies have confirmed the importance of search context in QC. (Cao et al., 2009) considered the context to be both previous queries within the same session and pages of the clicked urls. In our approach, we will also consider click through information to enrich the queries and analyze topics.

In (Le et al., 2011), queries and categories are enriched with both information mined from the click-through links as well as topics derived from a topic model estimated from the library metadata. Subsequently, the queries are mapped to the categories based on their cosine similarity. Our proposed approach differs from (Le et al., 2011) in three respects: (1) we enrich the queries, but not the categories (2) we employ a machine learning system and integrate this enriched information as features to learn an SVM classifier (3) we assume that the category of a query is closely related to the category of the corresponding click-through link, hence we automatically create a training data for the SVM classifier by analyzing the query log.

3 Bridgeman Art Library

Bridgeman Art Library (BAL)[2] is one of the world's top image libraries for art, culture and history. It contains images from over 8,000 collections and more than 29,000 artists, providing a central source of fine art for image users.

Works of art in the library have been annotated with titles and keywords. Some of them are categorized into a two-level taxonomy, a more fine-grained classification of the Bridgeman browse menu. In our study, we do not use the image itself but only the information associated with it, i.e., the title, keywords and categories. We will take the 55 top-level categories from this taxonomy, which have been organized by a domain expert, as our target taxonomy.

4 Building QC using topic models and SVM

Following (Le et al., 2011), we enrich queries both with the information mined from the library via click-through links and the information collected from the library metadata via topic modeling. To perform the query enrichment with topics derived from the library metadata, there are several important steps:

- Collecting and organizing the library metadata as a reference set: the library metadata contains the information about artworks that have been annotated by experts. To take advantage of this information automatically, we collected all annotated artworks and organized them by their given categories.
- Estimating a topic model for this reference set: This step is performed using hidden topic analysis models. In this framework, we choose to use latent dirichlet allocation, LDA (Blei et al., 2003b).
- Analyzing topics for queries and integrating topics into data for both the training set and new queries: After the reference set has been analyzed using topic models, it will be used to infer topics for queries. The topic model will then be integrated into the data to build a classifier.

4.1 Query enrichment via click-through links

We automatically extracted click-through links from the query log (which provides us with the title of the image that the user clicks) to enrich the query, represented as a vector $\overrightarrow{q_i}$, with the title of one randomly-chosen click-through associated with it. To further exploit the click-through link, we find the corresponding artwork and extract its keywords: $\overrightarrow{q_i} \cup \overrightarrow{t_i} \cup \overrightarrow{kw_i}$, where $\overrightarrow{t_i}$, $\overrightarrow{kw_i}$ are the vectors of words

[2]http://www.bridgemanart.com

in the title and keywords respectively.

4.2 Hidden Topic Models

The underlying idea is based upon a probabilistic procedure of generating a new set of artworks, where each set refers to titles and keywords of all artworks in a category: First, each set $\overrightarrow{w}_m = (w_{m,n})_{n=1}^{N_m}$ is generated by sampling a distribution over topics $\overrightarrow{\vartheta}_m$ from a Dirichlet distribution ($Dir(\overrightarrow{\alpha})$), where N_m is the number of words in that set m. After that, the topic assignment for each observed word $w_{m,n}$ is performed by sampling a word place holder $z_{m,n}$ from a multinomial distribution ($Mult(\overrightarrow{\vartheta_m})$). Then a word $w_{m,n}$ is picked by sampling from the multinomial distribution ($Mult(\overrightarrow{\varphi}_{z_{m,n}})$). This process is repeated until all K topics have been generated for the whole collection.

Table 1: Generation process for LDA

- M: the total number of artwork sets
- K: the number of (hidden/latent) topics
- V: vocabulary size
- $\overrightarrow{\alpha}$, $\overrightarrow{\beta}$: Dirichlet parameters
- $\overrightarrow{\vartheta}_m$: topic distribution for document m
- $\overrightarrow{\varphi}_k$: word distribution for topic k
- N_m: the length of document m
- $z_{m,n}$: topic index of nth word in document m
- $w_{m,n}$: a particular word for word placeholder [m, n]
- $\Theta = \{\overrightarrow{\vartheta}_m\}_{m=1}^{M}$: a $M \times K$ matrix
- $\Phi = \{\overrightarrow{\varphi}_k\}_{k=1}^{K}$: a $K \times V$ matrix

In order to estimate parameters for LDA (i.e., the set of topics and their word probabilities Φ and the particular topic mixture of each document Θ), different inference techniques can be used, such as variational Bayes (Blei et al., 2003b), or Gibbs sampling (Heinrich, 2004). In this work, we will use Gibbs sampling following the description given in (Heinrich, 2004). Generally, the topic assignment of a particular word t is computed as:

$$p(z_i = k | \overrightarrow{z}_{\neg i}, \overrightarrow{w}) = \frac{n_{k,\neg i}^{(t)} + \beta_t}{[\sum_{v=1}^{V} n_k^{(v)} + \beta_v] - 1} \frac{n_{m,\neg i}^{(k)} + \alpha_k}{[\sum_{j=1}^{K} n_m^{(j)} + \alpha_j] - 1} \quad (1)$$

where $n_{k,\neg i}^{(t)}$ is the number of times the word t is assigned to topic k except the current assignment; $\sum_{v=1}^{V} n_k^{(v)} - 1$ is the total number of words assigned to topic k except the current assignment; $n_{m,\neg i}^{(k)}$ is the number of words in set m assigned to topic k except the current assignment; and $\sum_{j=1}^{K} n_m^{(j)} - 1$ is the total number of words in set m except the current word t. In normal cases, Dirichlet parameters $\overrightarrow{\alpha}$, and $\overrightarrow{\beta}$ are symmetric, that is, all α_k (k = 1..K) are the same, and similarly for β_v (v = 1..V).

4.3 Hidden topic analysis of the Bridgeman metadata

The Bridgeman metadata contains information about artworks in the library that have been annotated by the librarians. We extracted titles and keywords of each artwork, those for which we had a query with a click-through link corresponding to it, and grouped them together by their sub-categories. Each group is considered as a document $\overrightarrow{w}_m = (w_{m,n})_{n=1}^{N_m}$, with the number of total documents M = 732 and the vocabulary size V = 136K words. In this experiment, we fix the number of topics K = 100. We used the GibbsLDA++ implementation[3] to estimate this topic model.

4.4 Building query classifier with hidden topics

Let $Q' = \{\overrightarrow{q_i}'\}_{i=1}^{i=N}$ be the set of all queries enriched via the click-through links, where each enriched query is $\overrightarrow{q_i}' = \overrightarrow{q_i} \cup \overrightarrow{t_i} \cup \overrightarrow{kw_i}$. We also performed Gibbs sampling for all $\overrightarrow{q_i}'$ in order to estimate its topic distribution $\overrightarrow{\vartheta}_i = \{\vartheta_{i,1}, \ldots, \vartheta_{i,K}\}$ where the probability $\vartheta_{i,k}$ of topic k in $\overrightarrow{q_i}'$ is computed as:

$$\vartheta_{i,k} = \frac{n_i^{(k)} + \alpha_k}{\sum_{j=1}^{K} n_i^{(j)} + \alpha_j} \quad (2)$$

where $n_i^{(k)}$ is the number of words in query i assigned to topic k and $n_i^{(j)}$ is the total number of words appearing in the enriched query i.

In order to integrate the topic distribution $\overrightarrow{\vartheta_i} = \{\vartheta_{i,1}, \ldots, \vartheta_{i,K}\}$ into the vector of words $\overrightarrow{q_i}' = \{w_{i,1}, w_{i,2}, \ldots, w_{i,N_i}\}$, following (Phan et al., 2010), we only keep topics whose $\vartheta_{i,k}$ is larger than a threshold *cut-off* and use a *scale* parameter to do the discretization for topics: the number of times topic k integrated to $\overrightarrow{q_i}'$ is round($\vartheta_i \times$ *scale*). After that, we build a Support Vector Machine classifier using SVM light V2.20[4].

[3] http://gibbslda.sourceforge.net/
[4] http://svmlight.joachims.org/

5 Evaluation

In this section, we will describe our training set, gold standard and the performance of our system in comparison with the one in (Le et al., 2011).

5.1 Training set

Manually annotating queries to create a training set in this domain is a difficult task (e.g., it requires the expert to search the query and look at the picture corresponding to the query, etc.). Therefore, we have automatically generated a training set by exploiting a 6-month query log as follow.

First, each query has been mapped to its click-through information to extract the sub-category associated to the corresponding image. Then, from this sub-category, we obtained its corresponding top-cateogry (among the 55 we consider) as defined in BAL taxonomy. The distribution of queries in different categories varies quite a lot among the 55 target categories reflecting the artwork distribution (e.g., there are many more artworks in the library belonging to the category "Religion and Belief" than to the category"Costume and Fashion"). We have preserved such distribution over the target categories when selecting randomly the 15,490 queries to build our training set. After removing all punctuations and stop words, we obtained a training set containing 50,337 words in total. Each word in this set serves as a feature for the SVM classifier.

5.2 Test set

We used the test set of 1,049 queries used in (Le et al., 2011), which is separate from the training set. These queries have been manually annotated by a BAL expert (up to 3 categories per query). Note that these queries have also been selected automatically while preserving the distribution over the target categories observed in the 6-month query log. We call this the "manual" gold standard. In addition, we also made use of another gold standard obtained by mapping the click-through information of these queries with their categories, similar to the way in which we obtain the training set. We call this the "via-CT" gold standard.

5.3 Experimental settings

To evaluate the impact of click-though information and topics in the classifier, we designed the following experiments, where QR is the method without any enrichment and $QR\text{-}CT\text{-}HT$ is with the enrichment via both click-through and hidden topics.

Setting	Query enrichment
QR	$\overrightarrow{q}$
$QR\text{-}HT$	$\overrightarrow{q} \oplus HT$
$QR\text{-}CT$	$\overrightarrow{q}' = \overrightarrow{q} + \overrightarrow{t} + \overrightarrow{kw}$
$QR\text{-}CT\text{-}HT$	$\overrightarrow{q}' \oplus HT$

- $\overrightarrow{q}$: query
- $\overrightarrow{q}'$: query enriched with click-through information
- $\overrightarrow{t}$: click-through image's title
- $\overrightarrow{kw}$: click-through image's keywords
- HT: hidden topics from Bridgeman metadata

Table 2: Experimental Setting

Setting	Hits				
	Manual GS				*via-CT*
	# 1	# 2	# 3	$\sum_{Top\_3}$	GS
QR	207	80	24	**311**	**231**
$QR\text{-}HT$	212	81	25	**318**	**235**
QR - CT	243	107	38	**388**	**266**
QR - CT - HT	289	136	49	**474**	**323**

Table 3: Results of query classification: number of correct categories found (for 1,049 queries)

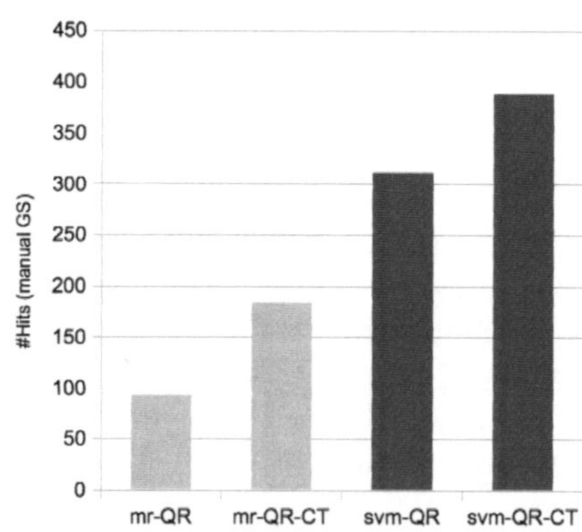

Figure 1: The impact of click-through information with matching-ranking (mr) and our approach (svm)

To answer our first research question, namely whether click-through information and hidden topics are useful for this query classifier, we examine the number of correct categories found by the classifier built both with and without the enrichment. The results of the experiment are reported in Table 3. As can be seen from the table, we notice that the click-through information plays an important role. In particular, it increases the number of correct categories found from 311 to 388 (compared with the *manual* GS) and from 231 to 266 (using the *via-CT* GS).

To answer our second research question, namely whether integrating the enriched information into a machine learning classifier can perform better than the matching and ranking method, we also compare the results of our approach with the one in (Le et al., 2011). Figure 1 shows the impact of the click-through information for the SVM classifier (svm) in comparison with the matching and ranking approach (mr). Figure 2 shows the impact of the hidden topics in both cases. We can see that in both cases our classifier outperforms the matching-ranking one considerably (e.g., from 183 to 388 correct categories found in the QR-CT-HT method).

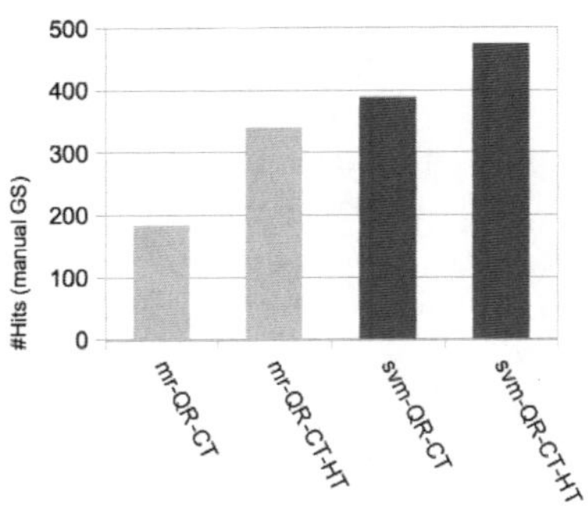

Figure 2: The impact of hidden topics with matching-ranking (mr) and our approach (svm)

However, in the case where we use only queries without click-through information, we can see that hidden topics do not bring a very strong impact (the number of correct categories found only slightly increases by 7 - using the "manual" gold standard). The result might come from the fact that this topic model was built from the metadata, using only click-through information, but has not been learned with queries.

6 Conclusion

In this study, we have presented a machine learning classifier for query classification in an art image archive. Since queries are usually very short, thus difficult to classify, we first extend them with their click-through information. Then, these queries are further enriched with topics learned from the BAL metadata following (Le et al., 2011). The result from this study has confirmed again the effect of click-through information and hidden topics in the query classification task using SVM. We have also described our method of automatically creating a training set based on the selection of queries mapped to the click-through links and their corresponding available categories using a 6-month query log. The result of this study has shown a considerable increase in the performance of this approach over the matching-ranking system reported in (Le et al., 2011).

7 Future work

For future work, we are in the process of enhancing our experimentation in several directions:

Considering more than one click-through image per query: In this work, we have considered only one category per query to create the training set, while it might be more reasonable to take into account all click-through images of a given query. In future work, we plan to enrich the queries with either all click-through images or with the most relevant one instead of randomly picking one click-through image. In many cases, a click-through link is not necessarily related to the meaning of a query (e.g., when users just randomly click on an image that they find interesting). Thus, it might be useful to filter out those click-through images that are not relevant.

Enriching queries with top hits returned by the BAL search engine: In the query logs, there are many queries that do not have an associated click-through link. Hence, we plan to exploit other enrichment method that do not rely on those links, in particular we will try to exploit the information coming from the top returned hits given by the library search engine.

Analyzing queries in the same session: It has been shown in some studies (Cao et al., 2009) that analyzing queries in the same session can help determine their categories. Our next step is to enrich a new query with the information coming from the other previous queries in the same session.

Optimizing LDA hyperparameters and topic number selection: Currently, we fixed the number of topics $K = 100$, the Dirichlet hyperparameters $\alpha = 50/K = 0.5$ and $\beta = 0.1$ as in (Griffiths and

Steyvers, 2004). In the future, we will explore ways to optimize these input values to see the effect of different topic models in our query classification task.

Exploiting visual features from the BAL images: The BAL dataset provides an interesting case study in which we plan to further analyze images to enrich queries with their visual features. Combining text and visual features has drawn a lot of attention in the IR research community. We believe that exploiting visual features from this art archive could lead to interesting results in this specific domain. A possible approach would be extracting visual features from the click-through images and representing them together with textual features in a joint topic distribution (e.g., (Blei et al., 2003a; Li et al., 2010)).

Comparing system with other approaches: In the future, we plan to compare our system with other query classification systems and similar techniques for query expansion in general. Furthermore, the evaluation phase has not been carried out thoroughly since it was difficult to compare the one-class output with the gold-standard, where the number of correct categories per query is not fixed. In the future, we plan to exploit the output of our multi-class classifier to assign up to three categories for each query and compute the precision at n.

Acknowledgments

This work has been partially supported by the GALATEAS project (http://www.galateas.eu/ – CIP-ICT PSP-2009-3-25430) funded by the European Union under the ICT PSP program.

References

Steven M. Beitzel, Eric C. Jensen, Ophir Frieder, and David Grossman. 2005. Automatic web query classification using labeled and unlabeled training data. In *In Proceedings of the 28th Annual International ACM SIGIR Conference on Research and Development in Information Retrieval*, pages 581–582. ACM Press.

David M. Blei, Michael I, David M. Blei, and Michael I. 2003a. Modeling annotated data. In *In Proc. of the 26th Intl. ACM SIGIR Conference*.

David M. Blei, Andrew Y. Ng, and Michael I. Jordan. 2003b. Latent dirichlet allocation. *J. Mach. Learn. Res.*, 3:993–1022, March.

Andrei Z. Broder, Marcus Fontoura, Evgeniy Gabrilovich, Amruta Joshi, Vanja Josifovski, and Tong Zhang. 2007. Robust classification of rare queries using web knowledge. In *Proceedings of the 30th annual international ACM SIGIR conference on Research and development in information retrieval*, SIGIR '07, pages 231–238, New York, NY, USA. ACM.

Andrei Broder. 2002. A taxonomy of web search. *SIGIR Forum*, 36:3–10, September.

Huanhuan Cao, Derek Hao Hu, Dou Shen, Daxi Jiang, Jian-Tao Sun, Enhong Chen, and Qiang Yang. 2009. Context-aware query classification. In *SIGIR'09, The 32nd Annual ACM SIGIR Conference.*

Thomas L Griffiths and Mark Steyvers. 2004. Finding scientific topics. *Proceedings of the National Academy of Sciences of the United States of America*, 101 Suppl 1(Suppl 1):5228–5235.

Gregor Heinrich. 2004. Parameter estimation for text analysis. Technical report.

Dieu-Thu Le, Raffaella Bernardi, and Edwin Vald. 2011. Query classification via topic models for an art image archive. In *Recent Advances in Natural Language Processing, RANLP, Bulgaria.*

Li-Jia Li, Chong Wang, Yongwhan Lim, David Blei, and Li Fei-Fei. 2010. Building and using a semantivisual image hierarchy. In *The Twenty-Third IEEE Conference on Computer Vision and Pattern Recognition*, San Francisco, CA, June.

Xuan-Hieu Phan, Cam-Tu Nguyen, Dieu-Thu Le, Le-Minh Nguyen, Susumu Horiguchi, and Quang-Thuy Ha. 2010. A hidden topic-based framework towards building applications with short web documents. *IEEE Transactions on Knowledge and Data Engineering*, 99(PrePrints).

Dou Shen, Rong Pan, Jian-Tao Sun, Jeffrey Junfeng Pan, Kangheng Wu, Jie Yin, and Giang Yang. 2006a. Query enrichment for web-query classification. *ACM Transactions on Information Systems*, 24(3):320–352.

Dou Shen, Jian-Tao Sun, Qiang Yang, and Zheng Chen. 2006b. Building bridges for web query classification. In *SIGIR'06*.

Evaluating Unsupervised Ensembles when applied to Word Sense Induction

Keith Stevens[1,2]
[1]University of California Los Angeles; Los Angeles , California, USA
[2]Lawrence Livermore National Lab; Livermore, California, USA*
kstevens@cs.ucla.edu

Abstract

Ensembles combine knowledge from distinct machine learning approaches into a general flexible system. While supervised ensembles frequently show great benefit, unsupervised ensembles prove to be more challenging. We propose evaluating various unsupervised ensembles when applied to the unsupervised task of Word Sense Induction with a framework for combining diverse feature spaces and clustering algorithms. We evaluate our system using standard shared tasks and also introduce new automated semantic evaluations and supervised baselines, both of which highlight the current limitations of existing Word Sense Induction evaluations.

1 Introduction

Machine learning problems often benefit from many differing solutions using ensembles (Dietterich, 2000) and supervised Natural Language Processing tasks have been no exception. However, use of unsupervised ensembles in NLP tasks has not yet been rigorously evaluated. Brody et al. (2006) first considered unsupervised ensembles by combining four state of the art Word Sense Disambiguation systems using a simple voting scheme with much success. Later, Brody and Lapata (2009) combined different feature sets using a probabilistic Word Sense Induction model and found that only some combinations produced an improved system. These early and limited evaluations show both the promise and drawback of combining different unsupervised models: particular combinations provide a benefit but selecting these combinations is non-trivial.

We propose applying a new and more general framework for combining unsupervised systems known as Ensemble Clustering to unsupervised NLP systems and focus on the fully unsupervised task of Word Sense Induction. Ensemble Clustering can combine together multiple and diverse clustering algorithms or feature spaces and has been shown to noticeably improve clustering accuracy for both text based datasets and other datasets (Monti et al., 2003; Strehl et al., 2002). Since Word Sense Induction is fundamentally a clustering problem, with many variations, it serves well as a NLP case study for Ensemble Clustering.

The task of Word Sense Induction extends the problem of Word Sense Disambiguation by simply assuming that a model must first learn and define a sense inventory before disambiguating multi-sense words. This induction step frees the disambiguation process from any fixed sense inventory and can instead flexibly define senses based on observed patterns within a dataset (Pedersen, 2006). However, this induction step has proven to be greatly challenging, in the most recent shared tasks, induction systems either appear to perform poorly or fail to outperform the simple Most Frequent Sense baseline (Agirre and Soroa, 2007a; Manandhar et al., 2010).

In this work, we propose applying Ensemble Clustering as a general framework for combining not only different feature spaces but also a variety of different clustering algorithms. Within this framework we will explore which types of models should be combined and how to best combine them. In addition, we propose two new evaluations: (1) new semantic coherence measures that evaluate the seman-

*This work was performed under the auspices of the U.S. Department of Energy by Lawrence Livermore National Laboratory under Contract DE-AC52-07NA27344 (LLNL-CONF-530791).

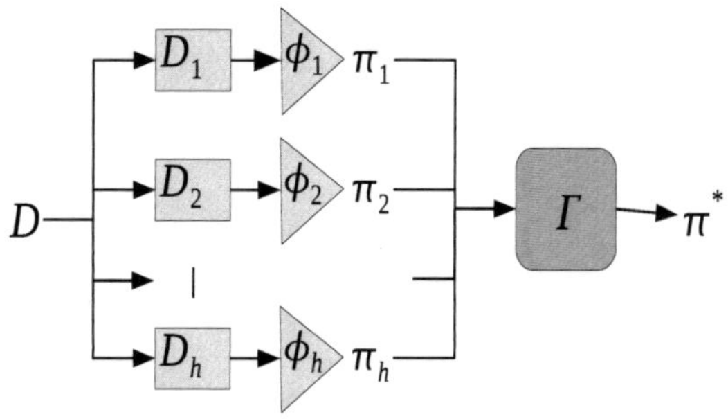

Figure 1: The Ensemble Clustering model: individual clustering algorithms partition perturbations of the dataset and all partitions are combined via a *consensus function* to create a final solution, π^*.

tic quality and uniqueness of induced word senses without referring to an external sense inventory (2) and a new set of baseline systems based on supervised learning algorithms. With the new evaluations and a framework for combining general induction models, we intend to find not only improved models but a better understanding of how to improve later induction models.

2 Consensus Clustering

Ensemble Clustering presents a new method for combining together arbitrary clustering algorithms without any supervision (Monti et al., 2003; Strehl et al., 2002). The method adapts simple boosting and voting approaches from supervised ensembles to merge together diverse clustering partitions into a single consensus solution. Ensemble Clustering forms a single consensus partition by processing a data set in two steps: (1) create a diverse set of ensembles that each partition some perturbation of the full dataset and (2) find the median partition that best agrees with each ensemble's partition. Figure 1 visually displays these two steps.

Variation in these two steps accounts for the wide variety of Ensemble Clustering approaches. Each ensemble can be created from either a large collection of distinct clustering algorithms or through a boosting approach where the same algorithm is trained on variations of the dataset. Finding the median partition turns out to be an NP-Complete problem under most settings (Goder and Filkov, 2008) and thus must be approximated with one of several heuristics. We consider several well tested approaches to both steps.

Formally, we define Ensemble Clustering to operate over a dataset of N elements: $D = \{d_1, \ldots, d_N\}$. Ensemble Clustering then creates H ensembles that each partition a perturbation D_h of D to create H partitions, $\Pi = \{\pi_1, \cdots, \pi_H\}$. The consensus algorithm then approximates the best consensus partition π^* that satisfies:

$$\underset{\pi^*}{\operatorname{argmin}} \sum_{\pi_h \in \Pi} d(\pi_h, \pi^*) \qquad (1)$$

according to some distance metric $d(\pi_i, \pi_j)$ between two partitions. We use the *symmetric difference distance* as $d(\pi_i, \pi_j)$. Let P_i be the set of co-cluster data points in π_i. The distance metric is then defined to be

$$d(\pi_1, \pi_2) = |P_1 \setminus P_2| + |P_2 \setminus P_1|$$

2.1 Forming Ensembles

Ensemble clustering can combine together overlapping decisions from many different clustering algorithms or it can similarly boost the performance of a single algorithm by using different parameters. We consider two simple formulations of ensemble creation: *Homogeneous Ensembles* and *Heterogeneous Ensembles*. We secondly consider approaches for combining the two creation methods.

Homogeneous Ensembles partition randomly sampled subsets of the data points from D without replacement. By sampling without replacement, each ensemble will likely see different representations of each cluster and can specialize its partition the around observed subset. Furthermore, each ensemble will observe less noise and can better define each true cluster (Monti et al., 2003). We note that since each ensemble only observes an incomplete subset of D, some clusters may not be represented at all in some partitions.

Heterogeneous Ensembles create diverse partitions by simply using complete partitions over D from different clustering algorithms, either due to different parameters or due to completely different clustering models (Strehl et al., 2002).

Combined Heterogeneous and Homogeneous Ensembles can be created by creating many homogeneous variations of each distinct clustering algorithm within a heterogeneous ensemble. In this framework, each single method can be boosted by subsampling the data in order to observe the true clusters and then combined with other algorithms using differing cluttering criteria.

2.2 Combining data partitions

Given the set of partitions, $\Pi = \{\pi_i, \cdots, \pi_h\}$, the consensus algorithm must find a final partition, π^* that best minimizes Equation 1. We find an approximation to π^* using the following algorithms.

Agglomerative Clustering first creates a *consensus matrix*, $\mathcal{M}$ that records the aggregate decisions made by each partition. Formally, $\mathcal{M}$ records the fraction of partitions that observed two data point *and* assigned them to the same cluster:

$$\mathcal{M}(i, j) = \frac{\sum_{k=1}^{h} 1\{d_i, d_j \in \pi_k^c\}}{\sum_{k=1}^{h} 1\{d_i, d_j \in \pi_k\}}$$

Where d_i refers to element i, π_k^c refers to cluster c in partition π_k, and $1\{*\}$ is the indicator function. The consensus partition, π^* is then the result of creating C partitions with Agglomerative Clustering using the Average Link criterion and $\mathcal{M}$ as the similarity between each data point (Monti et al., 2003).

Best of K simply sets π^* as the partition $\pi_h \in \Pi$ that minimizes Equation 1 (Goder and Filkov, 2008).

Best One Element Move begins with an initial consensus partition $\hat{\pi}^*$ and repeatedly changes the assignment of a single data point such that Equation 1 is minimized and repeats until no move can be found. We initialize this with Best of K.

Filtered Stochastic Best One Element Move also begins with an initial consensus partition $\hat{\pi}^*$ and repeatedly finds the best one element move, but does not compare against every partition in Π for each iteration. It instead maintains a history of move costs and updates that history with a stochastically selected partition from Π for each move iteration and ends after some fixed number of iterations (Zheng et al., 2011).

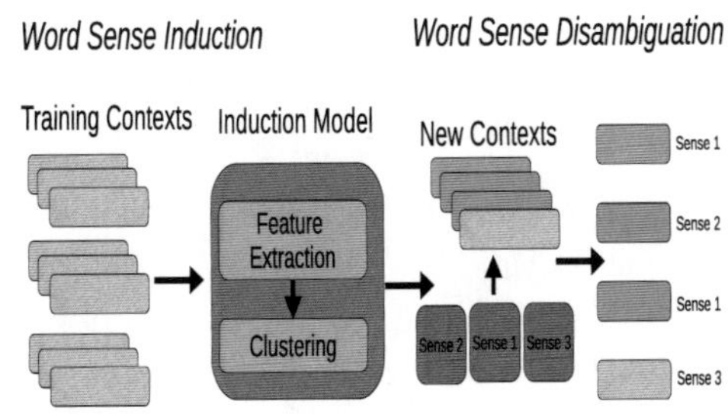

Figure 2: The general Word Sense Induction Model: models extract distributional data from contexts and induce senses by clustering the extracted information. Models then use representations of each sense to disambiguate new contexts.

3 Word Sense Induction Models

Word Sense Induction models define word senses in terms of the distributional hypothesis, whereby the meaning of a word can be defined by the surrounding context (Haris, 1985). Rather than form a single representation for any word, induction models represent the distinct contexts surrounding a multi-sense word and find commonalities between the observed contexts by clustering. These similar contexts then define a particular *word sense* and can be used to later recognize later instances of the sense, Figure 2.

Models can be roughly categorized based on their context model and their clustering algorithm into two categories: feature vector methods and graph methods. Feature vector methods simply transform each context into a feature vector that records contextual information and then cluster with any algorithm that can partition individual data points. Graph methods build a large distributional graph that models lexical features from all contexts and then partitions the graph using a graph-based clustering algorithm. In both cases, models disambiguate new uses of a word by finding the sense with the most features in common with the new context.

3.1 Context Models

Context models follow the distributional hypothesis by encoding various lexical and syntactic features that frequently occur with a multi-sense word. Each context model records different levels of information, and in different formats, but are limited to features available from syntactic parsing. Below we summarize our context models which are based on previous induction systems:

Word Co-occurence (WoC) acts as the core feature vector method and has been at the core of nearly all systems that model distributional semantics (Pedersen, 2006). The WoC model represents each context simply as the words within $\pm W$ words from the multi-sense word. Each co-occurring word is weighted by the number of times it occurs within the window.

Parts of Speech (PoS) extends the WoC model by appending each lexical feature with its part of speech. This provides a simple disambiguation of each feature so that words with multiple parts of speech are not conflated into the same feature. (Brody et al., 2006).

Dependency Relations (DR) restrains word co-occurrence to words that are reachable from the multi-sense word via a syntactic parse composed of dependency relationships limited by some length (Padó and Lapata, 2007). We treat each reachable word and the last relation in the path as a feature (Van de Cruys and Apidianaki, 2011).

Second Order Co-occurrence (SndOrd) provides a rough compositional approach to representing sentences that utilizes word co-occurrence and partially solves the data sparsity problem observed with the WoC model. The SndOrd model first builds a large distributional vector for each word in a corpus and then forms context vectors by adding the distributional vector for each co-occurring context word (Pedersen, 2006).

Graph models encode rich amounts of linguistic information for all contexts as a large distributional graph. Each co-occurring context word is assigned a node in the graph and edges are formed between any words that co-occur in the same context. The graph is refined by comparing nodes and edges to a large representative corpus and dropping some occurrences (Klapaftis and Manandhar, 2010).

Latent Factor Models projects co-occurrence information into a latent feature space that ties together relationships between otherwise distinct features. We consider three latent models: the Singular Value Decomposition (SVD) (Schütze, 1998), Non-negative Matrix Factorization (NMF) (Van de Cruys and Apidianaki, 2011), and Latent Dirichlet Allocation (Brody and Lapata, 2009). We note that SVD and NMF operate as a second step over any feature vector model whereas LDA is a standalone model.

3.2 Clustering Algorithms

Distributional clustering serves as the main tool for detecting distinct word senses. Each algorithm makes unique assumptions about the distribution of the dataset and should thus serve well as diverse models, as needed by supervised ensembles (Dietterich, 2000). While many WSI models automatically estimate the number of clusters for a word, we initially simplify our evaluation by assuming the number of clusters is known a priori and instead focus on the distinct underlying clustering algorithms. Below we briefly summarize each base algorithm:

K-Means operates over feature vectors and iteratively refines clusters by associating each context vector with its most representative centroid and then reformulating the centroid (Pedersen and Kulkarni, 2006).

Hierarchical Agglomerative Clustering can be applied to both feature vectors and collocation graphs. In both cases, each sentences or collocation vertex is placed in their own clusters and then the two most similar clusters are merged together into a new cluster (Schütze, 1998).

Spectral Clustering separates an associativity matrix by finding the cut with the lowest conductance. We consider two forms of spectral clustering: EigenCluster (Cheng et al., 2006), a method originally designed to cluster snippets for search results into semantically related categories, and GSpec (Ng et al., 2001), a method that directly clusters a collocation graph.

Random Graph Walks performs a series of random walks through a collocation graph in order to discover nodes that serve as central discriminative points in the graph and tightly connected components in the graph. We consider Chinese Whispers (Klapaftis and Manandhar, 2010) and a hub selection algorithm (Agirre and Soroa, 2007b).

4 Proposed Evaluation

We first propose evaluating ensemble configurations of Word Sense Induction models using the standard shared tasks from SemEval-1 (Agirre and Soroa, 2007a) and SemEval-2 (Manandhar et al., 2010). We then propose comparing these results, and past SemEval results, to supervised baselines as a gauge of how well the algorithms do compared to more informed models. We then finally propose an intrinsic evaluation that rates the semantic interpretability and uniqueness of each induced sense.

Evaluating Ensemble Configurations must be done to determine which variation of Ensemble Clustering best applies to the Word Sense Induction tasks. Preliminary research has shown that Homogeneous ensemble combined with the HAC consensus function typically improve base models while combining heterogeneous induction models *greatly* reduces performance. We thus propose various sets of ensembles to evaluate whether or not certain context models or clustering algorithms can be effectively combined:

1. mixing different feature vector models with the same clustering algorithm,
2. mixing different clustering algorithms using the same context model,
3. mixing feature vector context models and graph context models using matching clustering algorithms,
4. mixing all possible models,
5. and improving each heterogeneous algorithm by first boosting them with homogeneous ensembles.

SemEval Shared Tasks provide a shared corpus and evaluations for comparing different WSI Models. Both shared tasks from SemEval provide a corpus of training data for 100 multi-sense words and then compare the induced sense labels generated for a set of test contexts with human annotated sense using a fixed sense inventory. The task provides two evaluations: an *unsupervised* evaluation that treats each set of induced senses as a clustering solution and measures accuracy with simple metrics such as the Paired F-Score, V-Measure, and Adjusted Mutual Information; and a *supervised* evaluation that builds a simple supervised word sense disambiguation system using the sense labels (Agirre and Soroa, 2007a; Manandhar et al., 2010).

Supervised Baselines should set an upper limit on the performance we can expect from most unsupervised algorithms, as has been observed in other NLP tasks. We train these baselines by using feature vector models in combination with the SemEval-1 dataset[1]. We propose several standard supervised machine learning algorithms as different baselines: Naive Bayes, Logistic Regression, Decision Trees, Support Vector Machines, and various ensembles of each such as simple Bagged Ensembles.

Semantic Coherence evaluations balance the shared task evaluations by functioning without a sense inventory. Any evaluation against an existing inventory cannot accurately measure newly detected senses, overlapping senses, or different sense granularities. Therefore, our proposed *sense coherence* measures focus on the semantic quality of a sense, adapted from topic coherence measures (Newman et al., 2010; Mimno et al., 2011). These evaluate the degree to which features in an induced sense describe the meaning of the word sense, where highly related features constitute a more coherent sense and unrelated features indicate an incoherent sense. Furthermore, we adapt the coherence metric to evaluate the amount of semantic overlap between any two induced senses.

5 Concluding Remarks

This research will better establish the benefit of Ensemble Clustering when applied to unsupervised Natural Language Processing tasks that center around clustering by examining which feature spaces and algorithms can be effectively combined along with different different ensemble configurations. Furthermore, this work will create new baselines that evaluate the inherent challenge of Word Sense Induction and new automated and knowledge lean measurements that better evaluate new or overlapping senses learned by induction systems. All of the work will be provided as part of a flexible open source framework that can later be applied to new context models and clustering algorithms.

[1]We cannot use graph context models as they do not model contexts individually, nor can we use the SemEval-2 dataset because the training set lacks sense labels needed for training supervised systems

References

Eneko Agirre and Aitor Soroa. 2007a. Semeval-2007 task 02: evaluating word sense induction and discrimination systems. In *Proceedings of the 4th International Workshop on Semantic Evaluations*, SemEval '07, pages 7–12, Stroudsburg, PA, USA. Association for Computational Linguistics.

Eneko Agirre and Aitor Soroa. 2007b. Ubc-as: a graph based unsupervised system for induction and classification. In *Proceedings of the 4th International Workshop on Semantic Evaluations*, SemEval '07, pages 346–349, Stroudsburg, PA, USA. Association for Computational Linguistics.

Samuel Brody and Mirella Lapata. 2009. Bayesian word sense induction. In *Proceedings of the 12th Conference of the European Chapter of the Association for Computational Linguistics*, EACL '09, pages 103–111, Stroudsburg, PA, USA. Association for Computational Linguistics.

Samuel Brody, Roberto Navigli, and Mirella Lapata. 2006. Ensemble methods for unsupervised wsd. In *Proceedings of the 21st International Conference on Computational Linguistics and 44th Annual Meeting of the Association for Computational Linguistics*, pages 97–104, Sydney, Australia, July. Association for Computational Linguistics.

David Cheng, Ravi Kannan, Santosh Vempala, and Grant Wang. 2006. A divide-and-merge methodology for clustering. *ACM Trans. Database Syst.*, 31:1499–1525, December.

Thomas G. Dietterich. 2000. Ensemble methods in machine learning. In *Proceedings of the First International Workshop on Multiple Classifier Systems*, MCS '00, pages 1–15, London, UK. Springer-Verlag.

Andrey Goder and Valdimir Filkov, 2008. *Consensus Clustering Algorithms: Comparison and Refinement.*, pages 109–117.

Zellig Haris, 1985. *Distributional Structure*, pages 26–47. Oxford University Press.

Ioannis P. Klapaftis and Suresh Manandhar. 2010. Word sense induction & disambiguation using hierarchical random graphs. In *Proceedings of the 2010 Conference on Empirical Methods in Natural Language Processing*, EMNLP '10, pages 745–755, Stroudsburg, PA, USA. Association for Computational Linguistics.

Suresh Manandhar, Ioannis Klapaftis, Dmitriy Dligach, and Sameer Pradhan. 2010. Semeval-2010 task 14: Word sense induction & disambiguation. In *Proceedings of the 5th International Workshop on Semantic Evaluation*, pages 63–68, Uppsala, Sweden, July. Association for Computational Linguistics.

David Mimno, Hanna Wallach, Edmund Talley, Miriam Leenders, and Andrew McCallum. 2011. Optimizing semantic coherence in topic models. In *Proceedings of the 2011 Conference on Emperical Methods in Natural Language Processing*, pages 262–272, Edinburgh, Scotland, UK. Association of Computational Linguistics.

Stefano Monti, Pablo Tamayo, Jill Mesirov, and Todd Golub. 2003. Consensus clustering – a resampling-based method for class discovery and visualization of gene expression microarray data. *Machine Learning*, 52:91–118, July.

David Newman, Youn Noh, Edmund Talley, Sarvnaz Karimi, and Timothy Baldwin. 2010. Evaluating topic models for digital libraries. In *Proceedings of the 10th annual joint conference on Digital libraries*, JCDL '10, pages 215–224, New York, NY, USA. ACM.

A. Ng, M. Jordan, and Y. Weiss. 2001. On Spectral Clustering: Analysis and an algorithm. In T. Dietterich, S. Becker, and Z. Ghahramani, editors, *Advances in Neural Information Processing Systems*, pages 849–856. MIT Press.

Sebastian Padó and Mirella Lapata. 2007. Dependency-Based Construction of Semantic Space Models. *Computational Linguistics*, 33(2):161–199.

Ted Pedersen and Anagha Kulkarni. 2006. Automatic cluster stopping with criterion functions and the gap statistic. In *Proceedings of the 2006 Conference of the North American Chapter of the Association for Computational Linguistics on Human Language Technology: companion volume: demonstrations*, NAACL-Demonstrations '06, pages 276–279, Stroudsburg, PA, USA. Association for Computational Linguistics.

Ted Pedersen. 2006. Unsupervised corpus-based methods for WSD. In *Word Sense Disambiguation: Algorithms and Applications*, pages 133–166. Springer.

Hinrich Schütze. 1998. Automatic word sense discrimination. *Comput. Linguist.*, 24:97–123, March.

Alexander Strehl, Joydeep Ghosh, and Claire Cardie. 2002. Cluster ensembles - a knowledge reuse framework for combining multiple partitions. *Journal of Machine Learning Research*, 3:583–617.

Tim Van de Cruys and Marianna Apidianaki. 2011. Latent semantic word sense induction and disambiguation. In *Proceedings of the 49th Annual Meeting of the Association for Computational Linguistics: Human Language Technologies - Volume 1*, HLT '11, pages 1476–1485, Stroudsburg, PA, USA. Association for Computational Linguistics.

Haipeng Zheng, S.R. Kulkarni, and V.H. Poor. 2011. Consensus clustering: The filtered stochastic best-one-element-move algorithm. In *Information Sciences and Systems (CISS), 2011 45th Annual Conference on*, pages 1 –6, march.

Topic Extraction based on Prior Knowledge obtained from Target Documents

Kayo Tatsukawa and Ichiro Kobayashi
Advanced Sciences, Graduate School of Humanities and Sciences,
Ochanomizu University
2-1-1 Ohtsuka Bunkyo-ku Tokyo, 112-8610 JAPAN
{tatsukawa.kayo, koba}@is.ocha.ac.jp

Abstract

This paper investigates the relation between prior knowledge and latent topic classification. There are many cases where the topic classification done by Latent Dirichlet Allocation results in the different classification that humans expect. To improve this problem, several studies using Dirichlet Forest prior instead of Dirichlet distribution have been studied in order to provide constraints on words so as they are classified into the same or not the same topics. However, in many cases, the prior knowledge is constructed from a subjective view of humans, but is not constructed based on the properties of target documents. In this study, we construct prior knowledge based on the words extracted from target documents and provide it as constraints for topic classification. We discuss the result of topic classification with the constraints.

1 Introduction

We have recently faced situations in which we have to deal with a huge amount of text resources. To deal with these text resources, unlike studies to analyze the surface information of the resources, but a lot of studies to analyze latent semantics by means of Latent Dirichlet Allocation (LDA) (Blei et al., 2003) have been being studied. When extracting latent topics by means of LDA, there are many cases where the words naturally expected to be in the same topic are classified into different topics. To deal with this problem, several studies to provide a constraint for words to be in the same topic have been studied. Andrzejewski (Andrzejewski et al., 2009) has proposed a method to provide a constraint for topic clustering as prior knowledge consisting of the words, which should be in the same topic by applying Dirichlet Forest Prior as word probability distribution instead of Dirichlet distribution. However, in many cases, the prior knowledge is constructed from a subjective view of humans but is not automatically constructed based on the properties of target documents. In this study, we extract the words, which will be prior knowledge for extracting topics, from target documents, and provide it as a constraint for topic clustering, and then discuss the result of topic clustering with constraints on the words.

2 Related studies

Many studies to incorporate prior knowledge into topic models to raise the accuracy of topic clustering, introducing the techniques of semi-supervised learning(Andrzejewski et al., 2007; Andrzejewski et al., 2009; Andrzejewski and Zhu, 2009).

Andrzejewski (Andrzejewski et al., 2009) has incorporated a constraint on words into topic clustering by using Dirichlet Forest Prior instead of Dirichlet distribution. They have introduced 'Must-links' and 'Cannot-links', referring to the techniques of semi-supervised learning. 'Must-links' is a constraint that two words with similar probability distribution should be in the same topic. 'Cannot-links' is a constraint that two words with different probability distribution for all topics should be separated into different topics. Hu (Hu et al., 2011) has proposed a method which repeatedly extracts latent topics through the interaction with humans — constraints are added interactively by humans. In addition, Kobayashi (Kobayashi et al., 2011) has made it possible to use logical operation to combine the constraints, 'Must-links' and 'Cannot-links', in constructing prior knowledge. By this, they have proposed a method which can add new constraints constructed by logical operation of various constraints, and extract topics based on the constraints. In general, as for clustering with constraints, it is often that the constraints are given by humans. However, there are many cases where the constraints constructed by humans are arbitrary, in addition, it is laborious to construct prior knowledge for each target document. In this context, Kaji (Kaji et al., 2007) extracted synonyms from corpus by using vocabulary syntactic patterns and constructed prior knowledge for word clustering based on the synonyms. However, the method Kaji proposed obtains prior knowledge by learning approximately 1 billion corpus. So, it also costs much to construct the knowledge, furthermore, the obtained knowledge might be constraints for general purposes, but not for target documents. So, the constructed knowledge might not be appropriate for the target documents.

Considering these things, in this study, we use Dirichlet Forest Prior for word probability distribution and extract latent topics by the prior knowledge obtained from target documents, without using any big corpus. Then we will discuss how our method improves the accuracy of topic extraction.

3 Topic extraction by prior knowledge

3.1 Dirichlet Forest LDA

We use Dirichlet Forest prior (DF) as word probability distribution instead of Dirichlet distribution to reflect constraints on latent topic clustering. DF is hierarchical Dirichlet distribution and it uses α for topic distribution and β for word probability distribution as the hyper-parameters of Dirichlet distribution just like the conventional LDA. In addition, we use η which reflects the strength of given constraints on word occurrence distribution. In Dirichlet Forest, each leave has occurrence probability for each word and the sum of occurrence probability for all words becomes 1. In the process of generating a document with LDA using DF(LDA-DF), we firstly get a multinomial distribution θ with a hyper-parameter α, and then according to this multinomial distribution, a topic Z is selected. Secondly, we get a multinomial distribution ϕ with a hyper-parameter β, and then under the topic Z selected at θ, a word or a constraint is selected. If a word is selected, it is used directly to generate a document and if a constraint is selected, a word is selected according to a multinomial distribution π with hyper-parameter η.

Here, let d_i denote the documents which contain the i-th word w_i and z_i denote the topic which assigns on w_i. Using these parameters, LDA-DF is represented with the below equations.

$$\theta_{d_i} \sim \mathrm{Dirichlet}(\alpha) \quad (1)$$

$$z_i|\theta_{d_i} \sim \mathrm{Multinomial}(\theta_{d_i}) \quad (2)$$

$$q \sim \mathrm{DirichletForest}(\beta, \eta) \quad (3)$$

$$\phi_{z_i} \sim \mathrm{DirichletTree(q)} \quad (4)$$

$$w_i|z_i, \phi_{z_i} \sim \mathrm{Multinomial}(\phi_{z_i}) \quad (5)$$

3.2 Construction of prior knowledge

Newman (Newman et al., 2010) discusses various evaluation indices about the topic coherence. In this study, we choose Point-wise Mutual Information(PMI) as an index to measure topic coherence, and then estimate how much each obtained cluster increases topic coherence in itself. The reason why we choose PMI to measure topic coherence is based on the assumption that a topic is represented by the words with close relationship.

To construct prior knowledge, it is necessary to select words regarded as representatives of a topic. In this study, we assume that the words regarded as representatives of a topic ('important words', hereafter) frequently appear in all documents or have many co-occurrence relations with a lot of other words. We select important words by following the two basic ideas shown below.

(i) Important words based on frequency

In the case of dealing with multiple documents about the same topic, the words which frequently appear in all documents are regarded as necessary words to represent the contents of the documents. So, we regard such words as important words.

(ii) Important words based on co-occurrence

In this study, we construct prior knowledge as we suppose that a pair of words with high PMI value should be classified into the same topic. So, we regard the words, which have many co-occurrence relations with other words, as important words.

The prior knowledge is constructed by the following process.

step.1 Important words based on frequency or co-occurrence are selected.

step.2 Important words obtained at step.1 are classified into some groups based on co-occurrence relation. At this time, we use PMI as index to measure co-occurrence relation between words, and unite important words, which have higher PMI than the predefined threshold value, into a group.

step.3 Prior knowledge, i.e., the group obtained at step2, is constructed based on the words with high PMI values, therefore, the words which have high PMI value with the words in the group obtained at step.2 are further selected and added to the group, if necessary. Depending on the number of words added to the group, prior knowledge will be changed. So, we experiment to investigate the influence of the number of added words, changing the number of the words from 1 to 4. The detail about the experiment is mentioned in section 4.

4 Experiment

4.1 Experimental settings

As the documents for the experiment to extract topics, we used news articles about the same incident. The news articles we used are ABC News in USA, BBC News in UK, CTV News in Canada, which are published by main newspaper companies and TV companies in English-speaking countries.

We used the following 4 articles for the experiment: 10 articles about 'Press conference about the convergence of atomic power plant disaster by Japanese prime minister, 2011/12/16' consist of 212 documents and 853 terms; 24 articles about 'Grounding of pomp passenger ferry in Italy, 2012/1/16' consist of 967 documents and 2267 terms; 25 articles about 'Protest from Wikipedia to Stop Online Piracy Act (SOPA), 2012/1/16' consist of 700 documents and 1823 terms; 18 articles about 'Resignation of co-founder Yahoo!, 2012/1/16' consist of 553 documents and 1113 terms.

In the experiment, we used $\alpha = 0.1$, $\beta = 0.1$, $\eta = 100$ as hyper-parameters for LDA-DF and Collapsed Gibbs Sampling (Griffiths et al., 2004) for the presumption of probability distribution with 50 iteration times.

Although we could set the number of topics so as it fitted target documents by means of perplexity, since we aim to evaluate adequacy of grouping of words, adequacy of topic clustering in other words, in the same condition, so we conducted an experiment, setting the number of topics as 10 for all the target articles.

In Hu's study (Hu et al., 2011), in response to given words as constraints, they re-presumed latent topics by canceling a part of the topics already assigned to words by the topic model prior to addition of new constraints. They suggested 4 ways of selecting words to cancel a part of topics, and reported that in the 4 ways they got good results when new prior knowledge is added, topic assignment for all the words of the documents which include the words in the prior knowledge is once canceled and then applied again. Therefore, we also cancel the topics assigned to words in the same way of theirs.

We calculate the value of perplexity of topic distribution and compare the stability of a model between before and after giving constraints. we calculate perplexity with equation (6). Here, N is the number of all words in the target documents, w_{mn} is the n-th word in the m-th document; θ is occurrence probability of topic for the documents, and ϕ is occurrence probability of the words for every topic.

$$Perplexity(\boldsymbol{w}) = exp(-\frac{1}{N}\sum_{mn} log(\sum_{z} \theta_{mz}\phi_{zw_{mn}})) \tag{6}$$

4.2 Experiment result

Table 1 shows the groups of important words based on frequency and co-occurrence, and the words with high PMI score to the important words which are candidates to be added to the prior knowledge. We take up the article about 'Press conference about the convergence of atomic power plant disaster by Japanese prime minister' and explain how to interpret Table 1.

Looking at the intersection between the row of frequency and the column of 'Atomic plant'

Table 1: Groups of important words based on frequency or co-occurrence, and added words

Types/Articles		Atomic plant	Grounding of ferry	Protest to SOPA	Yahoo! co-founder
Frequency	grouping words	{prime,minister,reactor, fukushima} , {power,tokyo},{cold}, {nuclear},{plant}, {shutdown}.	{costa},{passenger}, {people}	{wikipedia},{online}, {piracy},{internet}	{yang},{board}, {yahoo},{company}, {thompson}
	added words	yoshihiko,electric,reached, noda,march,state	appears,unaccounted, friday	wale,stop,protect,free	bostock,position, chairman,struggling,scott
Co-occurrence	grouping words	{cooling,contaminated, water},{site},{year} {stable,state,response}, {worst,disaster}	{disaster,caused,sea}, {aground,ran},{gash}, {authority,safety}, {television},{evacuation}	{medium,industry,group, tech,information,popular}, {big},{legislation}, {service},{community}	{private,pursuing,deal, shareholder,asian}, {began},{leaving}, {resignation},{chief}, {medium}
	added words	ton,liquid,end,tank, chernobyl	technical,late,side, trained,human,survivor	social,web,proposed, provider,wale	large,university, struggling,thompson, scott,trading

in Table 1, the extracted important words were united to one group depending on the value of PMI, and then we obtained the following 6 groups: {prime, minister, reactor, fukushima},{power, tokyo},{cold},{nuclear},{plant},{shutdown}. After that, we added some words with high PMI value to each group to achieve the construction of prior knowledge. The words expected to be added to the groups are shown at the next row of grouping words. In fact, depending on the number of the words added to the groups of important words, prior knowledge will be changed and the result of topic clustering will also be changed. Furthermore, depending on the number of given constraints, the result of topic clustering will also be changed. Therefore, we examine how accuracy of topic clustering changes by means of perplexity as its index, increasing the number of given constraints one by one from the initial condition, i.e., without any constraint.

Here, we think that the values of PMI and perplexity will be changed by the combination of prior knowledge, however, in this study, we gave the constraints in the order of a group with higher PMI value.

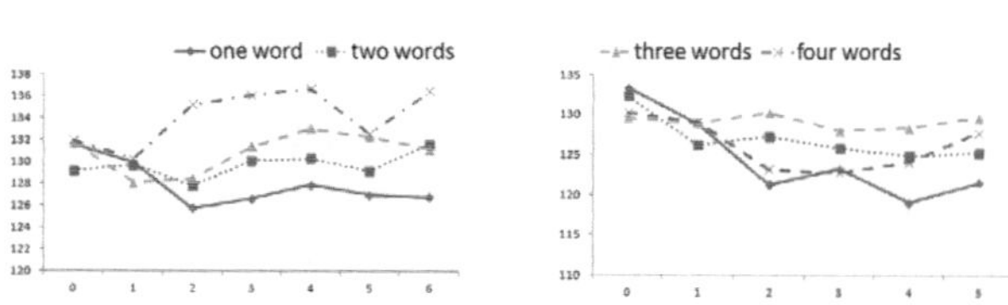

Frequency Co-occurrence

Figure 1: 'Convergence of atomic plant disaster'

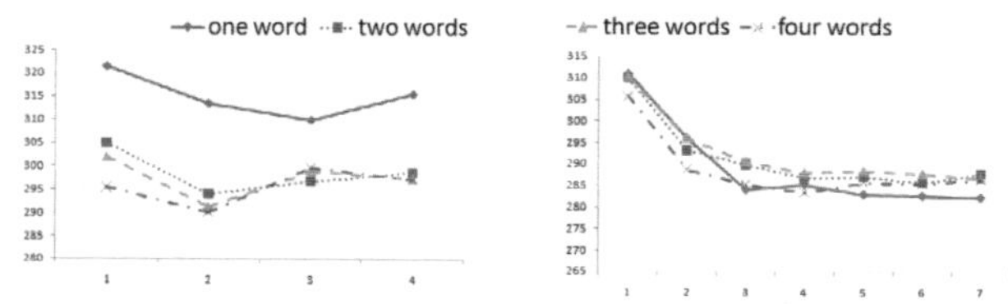

Frequency Co-occurrence

Figure 2: 'Grounding of pomp passenger ferry in Italy'

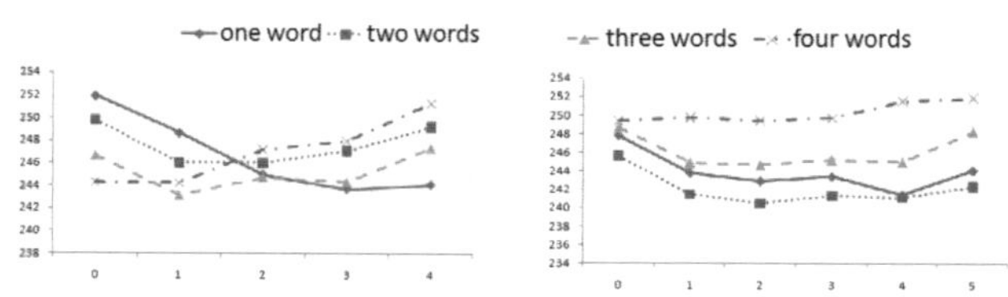

Frequency Co-occurrence

Figure 3: 'Protest of Wikipedia to SOPA'

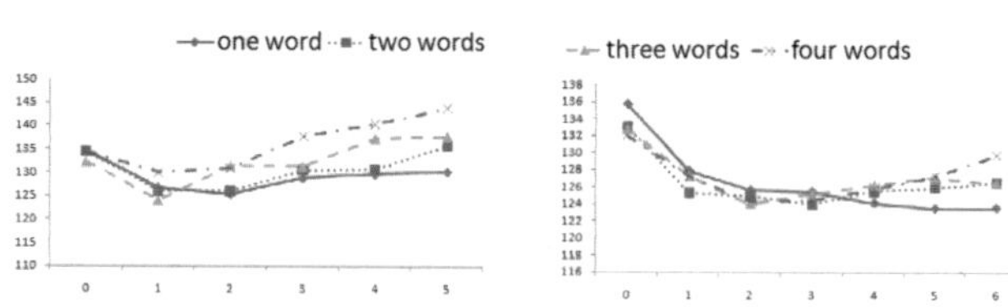

Frequency Co-occurrence

Figure 4: 'Resignation of Yahoo! co-founder'

Table 2: Top 10 representative words for topics extracted from the article 'Convergence of atomic plant disaster'

topic	topic0	topic1	topic2	topic3	topic4	topic5	topic6	topic7	topic8	topic9
LDA	water plant contaminated remains decade expert facility cool point problem	plant return home government zone resident remain evacuation mile doe	nuclear task told crisis meeting force disaster nod situation response	nuclear tsunami crisis march plant earthquake announcement fukushima meltdown month	cold shutdown reactor plant fukushima condition government stable power reached	accident nuclear disaster chernobyl university term country part engineering professor	tokyo electric power leak time week knocked huge bring official	year radiation plant area level government expected official start boundary	cooling minister reactor prime noda system degree yoshihiko nuclear temperature	reactor fuel tepco temperature rod melted spent inside damaged damage
topic	topic0	topic1	topic2	topic3	topic4	topic5	topic6	topic7	topic8	topic9
LDA-DF with constraints	facility waste tepco doe contaminated water including cooling earlier sea	plant home return mile zone government area resident official remain	nuclear noda task power force meeting japan set measure declared	tsunami plant march earthquake reactor crisis meltdown system daiichi people	cold shutdown plant reactor condition fukushima government reached friday radiation	nuclear cleanup university country significant disaster chernobyl worst term engineering	tokyo electric government power official told week bring company tepco	plant radiation level year end decade government decommission expert accident	nuclear prime minister degree announcement yoshihiko noda milestone mark news	reactor fuel temperature tepco rod fukushima melted cool spent inside

4.3 Discussions

We show the changes of perplexity in Figure 1, 2, 3, and 4 when increasing the number of constraints based on frequency and co-occurrence. In the Figures, the horizontal axis indicates the number of pieces of prior knowledge, and the vertical axis indicates the value of perplexity. Looking at these Figures, we see that the case of providing constraints based on co-occurrence decreases perplexity as the number of constraints increases, and the topic model becomes more stable than the case without constraint. Furthermore, we see that perplexity of each graph of co-occurrence can be decreased if providing one or two additional words with high value of PMI as a part of prior knowledge, and also that perplexity becomes stable when approximately 3 constraints are provided. From these observations, we think that we do not have to provide so many constraints to get good topic clustering.

On the other hand, unlike the case of providing constraints based on co-occurrence, we cannot get a general view for the case of providing constraints based on frequency from the results.

The reason why we could get good results when providing constraints based on co-occurrence information is that we constructed the prior knowledge which simultaneously reflects both 'Must-Links' and 'Cannot-Links' used as prior knowledge in (Andrzejewski et al., 2009), because PMI represents the co-occurrence relation of words in a sentence, so we think that it could divide the words should be included or should not be included in a topic.

On the other hand, we also see the case where perplexity gets increased even if selecting important words based on co-occurrence. Looking at the case of providing four additional words to prior knowledge in the graph of co-occurrence, especially in Figure 2,3,and 4, we see that perplexity increases as the number of pieces prior knowledge increases. We think the reason for this is because we added words to prior knowledge in the order of high PMI value, so the fourth word should not have had high PMI value, therefore, topic clusters became unstable.

Table 2 shows the result of topic classification of the article about 'Press conference of the convergence of atomic power plant disaster by Japanese prime minister.' We added the following constraints as prior knowledge: {worst, disaster, chernobyl},{cooling, contaminated, water, ton}, and {year, end} which is constructed based on co-occurrence information in the objective article. The upper row of Table 2 is the result of the conventional LDA without any constraint and the lower row is that of LDA-DF with constraints.

We see from Table 2 that the words consisting of

prior knowledge are split into two topics at the upper row, whereas, they are classified in the same topic, i.e., topic 0,5,and 7 at the lower row. We see that topic clustering with the constraints has been well achieved.

5 Conclusion

The conventional LDA sometimes results in topic classification different from what humans expect. To improve this, several studies providing constraints for topic clustering have been studied, referring to the techniques of semi-supervised learning.

In this study, we have constructed prior knowledge, which becomes constraints for topic clustering, with target documents which topics are extracted, unlike the studies to construct the knowledge with huge corpus. The prior knowledge will be constructed as a collection of the words expected to be representative of a topic. Based on this, we have introduced two ways to construct the knowledge: one is to select important words based on frequency and the other is to select words based on co-occurrence from target documents. We have compared the results of topic clustering by giving the two types of prior knowledge, and then recognized that the result of topic clustering based on the prior knowledge constructed based on co-occurrence is better than that by the prior knowledge constructed based on frequency. Furthermore, we have also investigated how much prior knowledge should be given as constraints for good topic clustering, and then obtained a result that good clustering is achieved even with a few pieces of prior knowledge, if the prior knowledge is constructed based on word co-occurrence. However, we have also observed several cases where this result cannot be correct. We need more investigation about this, revising the way of constructing prior knowledge. For future work, we will investigate another possibility to construct prior knowledge, and will apply our proposed method to various kinds of many documents.

References

David M. Blei and Andrew Y. Ng and Michael I. Jordan and John Lafferty. 2003. *Latent dirichlet allocation*, Journal of Machine Learning Research,

Hayato Kobayashi and Hiromi Wakaki and Tomohiro Yamasaki and Masaru Suzuki 2011. *Topic Models with Logical Constraints on Words*, Proc. of Workshop on Robust Unsupervised and Semisupervised Methods in Natural Language Processing,

Andrzejewski, Anne Mulhern, Ben Liblit, and Xiaojin Zhu, 2007. *Statistical Debugging Using Latent Topic Models*, Proceedings of the 18th European Conference on Machine Learning (ECML2007), pp. 6–17, Springer-Verlag.

Andrzejewski, David and Zhu, Xiaojin and Craven, Mark, 2009. *Incorporating domain knowledge into topic modeling via Dirichlet Forest priors*, Proceedings of the 26th Annual International Conference on Machine Learning. ICML '09, pp. 25–32, Montreal, Quebec, Canada.

Andrzejewski, David and Zhu, Xiaojin, 2009. *Dirichlet Allocation with Topic-in-Set Knowledge* Proceedings of NAACL-HLT2009 Workshop on Semi-Supervised Learning for Natural Language Processing, pp. 43–48.

Hu, Yuening and Boyd-Graber, Jordan and Satinoff, Brianna, 2011. *Interactive topic modeling*, Proceedings of the 49th Annual Meeting of the Association for Computational Linguistics: Human Language Technologies - Volume 1, pp.248–257, Portland, Oregon, USA.

Nobuhiro Kaji and Masaru Kitsuregawa, 2007. *Constrained distributional clustering of words using lexico-syntactic patterns (in Japanese)*, SIG-KBS, 79, pp.61-66, 2007-12-03.

Newman, David and Lau, Jey Han and Grieser, Karl and Baldwin, Timothy, 2010. *Automatic evaluation of topic coherence*, Human Language Technologies: The 2010 Annual Conference of the North American Chapter of the Association for Computational Linguistics, pp. 100–108,Los Angeles, California.

S.Y.Dennis III. 1991. *On the Hyper-Dirichlet Type 1 and Hyper-Liouville distributions.*, Communications in Statics – Theory and Methods 20(12):pp.4069-4081.

Minka, T.P. 1999. *The Dirichlet-tree distribution*, (Technical Report) http://research.microsoft.com/en-us/um/people/minka/papers/dirichlet/minka-dirtree.pdf

Kristina Toutanova and Mark Johnson. 2008. *A Baysian LDA-based model for semi-supervised part-of-speech tagging.*, In Advances in Neural Information Processing Systems 20, pp.1521-1528, MIT Press.

Thomas L.Griffiths and Mark Steyvers. 2004. *Finding scientific topics*, Proceedings of the National Academy of Sciences, Vol.101,No.Suppl 1. pp.5228-5235.

TopicTiling: A Text Segmentation Algorithm based on LDA

Martin Riedl and **Chris Biemann**
Ubiquitous Knowledge Processing Lab
Computer Science Department, Technische Universität Darmstadt
Hochschulstrasse 10, D-64289 Darmstadt, Germany
{riedl,biemann}@cs.tu-darmstadt.de

Abstract

This work presents a Text Segmentation algorithm called *TopicTiling*. This algorithm is based on the well-known TextTiling algorithm, and segments documents using the *Latent Dirichlet Allocation (LDA)* topic model. We show that using the mode topic ID assigned during the inference method of LDA, used to annotate unseen documents, improves performance by stabilizing the obtained topics. We show significant improvements over state of the art segmentation algorithms on two standard datasets. As an additional benefit, TopicTiling performs the segmentation in linear time and thus is computationally less expensive than other LDA-based segmentation methods.

1 Introduction

The task tackled in this paper is Text Segmentation (TS), which is to be understood as the segmentation of texts into topically similar units. This implies, viewing the text as a sequence of subtopics, that a subtopic change marks a new segment. The challenge for a text segmentation algorithm is to find the sub-topical structure of a text.

In this work, this semantic information is gained from Topic Models (TMs). We introduce a newly developed TS algorithm called *TopicTiling*. The core algorithm is a simplified version of *TextTiling* (Hearst, 1994), where blocks of text are compared via bag-of-word vectors. *TopicTiling* uses topic IDs, obtained by the LDA inference method, instead of words. As some of the topic IDs obtained by the inference method tend to change for different runs, we recommend to use the most probable topic ID assigned during the inference. We denote this most probable topic ID as the mode (most frequent across all inference steps) of the topic assignment. These IDs are used to calculate the cosine similarity between two adjacent blocks of sentences, represented as two vectors, containing the frequency of each topic ID. Without parameter optimization we obtain state-of-the-art results based on the Choi dataset (Choi, 2000). We show that the mode assignment improves the results substantially and improves even more when parameterizing the size of sampled blocks using a window size parameter. Using these optimizations, we obtain significant improvements compared to other algorithms based on the Choi dataset and also on a more difficult Wall Street Journal (WSJ) corpus provided by Galley et al. (2003). Not only does TopicTiling deliver state-of-the-art segmentation results, it also performs the segmentation in linear time, as opposed to most other recent TS algorithms.

The paper is organized as follows: The next section gives an overview of text segmentation algorithms. Section 3 introduces the TopicTiling TS algorithm. The Choi and the Galley datasets used to measure the performance of TopicTiling are described in Section 4. In the evaluation section, the results of TopicTiling are demonstrated on these datasets, followed by a conclusion and discussion.

2 Related Work

TS can be divided into two sub-fields: (i) linear TS and (ii) hierarchical TS. Whereas linear TS deals with the sequential analysis of topical changes, hierarchical segmentation is concerned with finding more fine grained subtopic structures in texts. One of the first unsupervised linear TS algorithms was introduced by Hearst (1994): *TextTiling* segments texts in linear time by calculating the similarity between two blocks of words based on the cosine similarity. The calculation is accomplished by two vectors containing the number of occurring terms of each block. *LcSeg* (Galley et al., 2003), a TextTiling-based algorithm, uses tf-idf term weights and improved TS results compared to TextTiling. Utiyama and Isahara (2001) introduced one of the first probabilistic approaches using Dynamic Programming (DP) called *U00*. Related to our work are the DP approaches described in Misra et al. (2009) and Sun et al. (2008): here, topic modeling is used to alleviate the sparsity of word vectors. This approach was extended by (Misra et al., 2009) and (Sun et al., 2008) using topic information achieved from the LDA topic model. The first hierarchical algorithm was proposed by Yaari (1997), using the cosine similarity and agglomerative clustering approaches. A hierarchical Bayesian algorithm based on LDA is introduced with Eisenstein (2009). In our work, however, we focus on linear TS.

LDA was introduced by Blei et al. (2003) and is a generative model that discovers topics based on a training corpus. Model training estimates two distributions: A topic-word distribution and a topic-document distribution. As LDA is a generative probabilistic model, the creation process follows a generative story: First, for each document a topic distribution is sampled. Then, for each document, words are randomly chosen, following the previously sampled topic distribution. Using the Gibbs inference method, LDA is used to apply a trained model for unseen documents. Here, words are annotated by topic IDs by assigning a topic ID sampled by the document-word and word-topic distribution. Note that the inference procedure, in particular, marks the difference between LDA and earlier dimensionality reduction techniques such as Latent Semantic Analysis.

3 TopicTiling

This section introduces the *TopicTiling* algorithm, first introduced in (Riedl and Biemann, 2012a). In contrast to the quite similar TextTiling algorithm, TopicTiling is not based on words, but on the last topic IDs assigned by the Bayesian Inference method of LDA. This increases sparsity since the word space is reduced to a topic space of much lower dimension. Therefore, the documents that are to be segmented have first to be annotated with topic IDs. For useful topic distinctions, however, the topic model must be trained on documents similar in content to the test documents. Preliminary experiments have shown that repeating the Bayesian inference, often leads to different topic distributions for a given sentence in several runs. Memorizing each topic ID assigned to a word in a document during each inference step can alleviate this instability, which is rooted in the probabilistic nature of LDA. After finishing the inference on the unseen documents, we select the most frequent topic ID for each word and assign it to the word. We call this method the mode of a topic assignment, denoted with $d = true$ in the remainder (Riedl and Biemann, 2012b). Note that this is different from using the overall topic distribution as determined by the inference step, since this winner-takes-it-all approach reduces noise from random fluctuations. As this parameter stabilizes the topic IDs at low computational costs, we recommend using this option in all setups where subsequent steps rely on a single topic assignment.

TopicTiling assumes a sentence s_i as the smallest basic unit. At each position p, located between two adjacent sentences, a *coherence score* c_p is calculated. With w we introduce a so-called *window parameter* that specifies the number of sentences to the left and to the right of position p that define two *blocks*: $s_{p-w}, \ldots, s_p$ and $s_{p+1}, \ldots, s_{p+w+1}$. In contrast to the mode topic assignment parameter d, we cannot state a recommended value for w, as this parameter is dependent on the number of sentences a segment should contain. This is conditioned on the corpus that is segmented.

To calculate the coherence score, we exclusively use the topic IDs assigned to the words by inference: Assuming an LDA model with T topics, each block is represented as a T-dimensional vector. The t-th element of each vector contains the frequency of the topic ID t obtained from the according block. The coherence score is calculated by the vector dot product, also referred to as *cosine similarity*. Values close to zero indicate marginal relatedness between two adjacent blocks, whereas values close to one denote a substantial connectivity. Next, the coherence scores are plotted to trace the local minima. These minima are utilized as possible segmentation boundaries. But rather using the c_p values itself, a *depth score* d_p is calculated for each minimum (cf. TextTiling, (Hearst, 1994)). In comparison to TopicTiling, TextTiling calculates the depth score for each position and than searches for maxima. The depth score measures the deepness of a minimum by looking at the highest coherence scores on the left and on the right and is calculated using following formula: $d_p = 1/2(hl(p) - c_p + hr(p) - c_p)$.

The function $hl(p)$ iterates to the left as long as the score increases and returns the highest coherence score value. The same is done, iterating in the other direction with the $hr(p)$ function. If the number of segments n is given as input, the n highest depth scores are used as segment boundaries. Otherwise, a threshold is applied (cf. TextTiling). This threshold predicts a segment if the depth score is larger than $\mu - \sigma/2$, with μ being the mean and σ being the standard variation calculated on the depth scores.

The algorithm runtime is linear in the number of possible segmentation points, i.e. the number of sentences: for each segmentation point, the two adjacent blocks are sampled separately and combined into the coherence score. This, and the parameters d and w, are the main differences to the dynamic programming approaches for TS described in (Utiyama and Isahara, 2001; Misra et al., 2009).

4 Data Sets

The performance of the introduced algorithm is demonstrated using two datasets: A dataset proposed by Choi and another more challenging one assembled by Galley.

4.1 Choi Dataset

The Choi dataset (Choi, 2000) is commonly used in the field of TS (see e.g. (Misra et al., 2009; Sun et al., 2008; Galley et al., 2003)). It is a corpus, generated artificially from the Brown corpus and consists of 700 documents. For document generation, ten segments of 3-11 sentences each, taken from different documents, are combined forming one document. 400 documents consist of segments with a sentence length of 3-11 sentences and there are 100 documents each with sentence lengths of 3-5, 6-8 and 9-11.

4.2 Galley Dataset

Galley et al. (2003) present two corpora for written language, each having 500 documents, which are also generated artificially. In comparison to Choi's dataset, the segments in its 'documents' vary from 4 to 22 segments, and are composed by concatenating full source documents. One dataset is generated based on WSJ documents of the Penn Treebank (PTB) project (Marcus et al., 1994) and the other is based on Topic Detection Track (TDT) documents (Wayne, 1998). As the WSJ dataset seems to be harder (consistently higher error rates across several works), we use this dataset for experimentation.

5 Evaluation

The performance of TopicTiling is evaluated using two measures, commonly used in the TS task: The P_k measure and the WindowDiff (WD) measure (Beeferman et al., 1999; Pevzner and Hearst, 2002). Besides the training corpus, the following parameters need to be specified for LDA: The number of topics T, the number of sample iterations for the model m and two hyperparameters α and β, specifying the sparseness of the topic-document and the topic-word distribution. For the inference method, the number of sampling iterations i is required. In line with Griffiths and Steyvers (2004), the following standard parameters are used: $T = 100$, $\alpha = 50/T$, $\beta = 0.01$, $m = 500$, $i = 100$. We use the JGibbsLDA implementation described in Phan and Nguyen (2007).

5.1 Evaluation of the Choi Dataset

For the evaluation we use a 10-fold Cross Validation (CV): the full dataset of 700 documents is split into 630 documents for training the topic model and 70 documents that are segmented. These two steps are repeated ten times to have all 700 documents segmented. For this dataset, no part-of-speech based word filtering is necessary. The results for different parameter settings are listed in Table 1.

When using only the window parameter without the mode (d=false), the results demonstrate a sig-

seg. size	3-5		6-8		9-11		3-11	
	P_k	WD	P_k	WD	P_k	WD	P_k	WD
d=false,w=1	2.71	3.00	3.64	4.14	5.90	7.05	3.81	4.32
d=true,w=1	3.71	4.16	1.97	2.23	2.42	2.92	2.00	2.30
d=false,w=2	1.46	1.51	1.05	1.20	1.13	1.31	1.00	1.15
d=true,w=2	**1.24**	**1.27**	**0.76**	**0.85**	**0.56**	**0.71**	**0.95**	**1.08**
d=false,w=5	2.78	3.04	1.71	2.11	4.47	4.76	3.80	4.46
d=true,w=5	2.34	2.65	1.17	1.35	4.39	4.56	3.20	3.54

Table 1: Results based on the Choi dataset with varying parameters.

nificant error reduction when using a window of 2 sentences. An impairment is observed when using a too large window (w=5). This is expected, as the size of the segments is in a range of 3-11 sentences: A window of 5 sentences therefore leads to blocks that contain segment boundaries. We can also see that the mode method improves the results when using a window of one, except for the documents having small segments ranging from 3-5 sentences. The lowest error rates are obtained with the mode method and a window size of 2.

As described above, the algorithm is also able to automatically estimate the number of segments using a threshold value (see Table 2).

	3-5		6-8		9-11		3-11	
	P_k	WD	P_k	WD	P_k	WD	P_k	WD
d=false,w=1	**2.39**	**2.45**	4.09	5.85	9.20	15.44	4.87	6.74
d=true,w=1	3.54	3.59	1.98	2.57	3.01	5.15	2.04	2.62
d=false,w=2	15.53	15.55	0.79	0.88	1.98	3.23	1.03	1.36
d=true,w=2	14.65	14.69	**0.62**	**0.62**	**0.67**	**0.88**	**0.66**	**0.78**
d=false,w=5	21.47	21.62	16.30	16.30	6.01	6.14	14.31	14.65
d=true,w=5	21.57	21.67	17.24	17.24	6.44	6.44	15.51	15.74

Table 2: Results on the Choi dataset without given number of segments as parameter.

The results show that for small segments, the number of segments is not correctly estimated, as the error rates are much higher than with given segments. As the window parameter has a smoothing effect on the coherence score function, less possible boundary candidates are detected. We can also see that the usage of the mode parameter leads to worse results with w=1 compared to the results where the mode is deactivated for the documents containing segments of length 3-5. Especially, results on these documents suffer when not providing the number of segments. But for the other documents, results are much better. Some results (see segment lengths 6-8 and 3-11 with d=true and w=2) are even better than the results with segments provided (see Table 1). The threshold method can outperform the setup with given a number of segments, since not recognizing a segment produces less error in the measures than predicting a wrong segment.

Table 3 presents a comparison of the performance of TopicTilig compared to different algorithms in the literature.

Method	**3-5**	**6-8**	**9-11**	**3-11**
TT (Choi, 2000)	44	43	48	46
C99 (Choi, 2000)	12	9	9	12
U00 (Utiyama and Isahara, 2001)	9	7	5	10
LCseg (Galley et al., 2003)	8.69			
F04 (Fragkou et al., 2004)	5.5	3.0	1.3	7.0
M09 (Misra et al., 2009)	2.2	2.3	4.1	2.3
TopicTiling (d=true, w=2)	**1.24**	**0.76**	**0.56**	**0.95**

Table 3: Lowest P_k values for the Choi data set for various algorithms in the literature with number of segments provided

It is obvious that the results are far better than current state-of-the-art results. Using a one-sampled t-test with $\alpha = 0.05$ we can state significant improvements in comparison to all other algorithms.

While we aim not using the same documents for training and testing by using a CV scheme, it is not guaranteed that all testing data is unseen, since the same source sentences can find their way in several artificially crafted 'documents'. We could detect reoccurring snippets in up to 10% of the documents provided by Choi. This problem, however, applies for all evaluations on this dataset that use any kind of training, be it LDA models in Misra et al. (2009) or tf-idf values in Fragkou et al. (2004) and Galley et al. (2003).

5.2 Evaluation on Galley's WSJ Dataset

For the evaluation on Galley's WSJ dataset, a topic model is created from the WSJ collection of the PTB project. The dataset for model estimation consists of 2499 WSJ articles, and is the same dataset Galley used as a source corpus. The evaluation generally leads to higher error rates than in the evaluation for the Choi dataset, as shown in Table 4.

This table shows results of the WSJ data when using all words of the documents for training a topic model and assigning topic IDs to new documents and also filtered results, using only nouns (proper

Parameters	All words		Filtered	
	P_k	WD	P_k	WD
d=false,w=1	37.31	43.20	37.01	43.26
d=true,w=1	35.31	41.27	33.52	39.86
d=false,w=2	22.76	28.69	21.35	27.28
d=true,w=2	21.79	27.35	19.75	25.42
d=false,w=5	14.29	19.89	12.90	18.87
d=true,w=5	**13.59**	**19.61**	**11.89**	**17.41**
d=false,w=10	14.08	22.60	14.09	22.22
d=true,w=10	13.61	21.00	13.48	20.59

Table 4: Results for Galley's WSJ dataset using different parameters with using unfiltered documents and with filtered documents using only verbs, nouns (proper and common) and adjectives.

and common), verbs and adjectives[1]. Considering the unfiltered results we observe that results improve when using the mode assigned topic ID and a window of larger than one sentence. In case of the WSJ dataset, we find the optimal setting for w=5. As the test documents contain whole articles, which consist of at least 4 sentences, a larger window is advantageous here, yet a value of 10 is too large. Filtering the documents for parts of speech leads to $\sim$ 1% absolute error rate reduction, as can be seen in the last two columns of Table 4. Again, we observe that the mode assignment always leads to better results, gaining at least 0.6%. Especially the window size of 5 helps TopicTiling to decrease the error rate to a third of the value observed with d=false and w=1. Similar to the previous findings, results decline when using a too large window.

Table 5 shows the results we achieve with the threshold-based estimation of segment boundaries for the unfiltered and filtered data.

Parameters	All words		Filtered	
	P_k	WD	P_k	WD
d=false,w=1	53.07	72.78	52.63	72.66
d=true,w=1	53.42	74.12	51.84	72.57
d=false,w=2	46.68	65.01	44.81	63.09
d=true,w=2	46.08	64.41	43.54	61.18
d=false,w=5	30.68	43.73	28.31	40.36
d=true,w=5	28.29	38.90	26.96	36.98
d=false,w=10	19.93	32.98	18.29	29.29
d=true,w=10	**17.50**	**26.36**	**16.32**	**24.75**

Table 5: Table with results the WSJ dataset without number of segments given, using all words and content words only.

[1]The Treetagger `http://code.google.com/p/tt4j/` is applied to POS-tag the data

In contrast to the results obtained with the Choi dataset (see Table 2) no decline is observed when the threshold approach is used in combination with the window approach. We attribute this due to the small segments and documents used in the Choi setting. Comparing the all-words data with pos-filtered data, an improvement is always observed. Also a continuous decreasing of both error rates, P_k and WD, is detected when using the mode and using a larger window size, even for w=10. The reason for this is that too many boundaries are detected when using small windows. As the window approach smoothes the similarity scores, this leads to less segmentation boundaries, which improve results.

For comparison, we present the evaluation results of other algorithms, shown in Table 6, as published in Galley et al. (2003).

Method	P_k	WD
C99 (Choi, 2000)	19.61	26.42
U00 (Utiyama and Isahara, 2001)	15.18	21.54
LCseg (Galley et al., 2003)	12.21	18.25
TopicTiling (d=true,w=5)	**11.89**	**17.41**

Table 6: List of results based on the WSJ dataset. Values for C99, U00 and LCseg as stated in (Galley et al., 2003).

Again, TopicTiling improves over the state of the art. The improvements with respect to LCseg are significant using a one-sample t-test with $\alpha = 0.05$.

6 Conclusion and Further Work

We introduced *TopicTiling*, a new TS algorithm that outperforms other algorithms as shown on two datasets. The algorithm is based on TextTiling and uses the topic model LDA to find topical changes within documents. A general result with implications to other algorithms that use LDA topic IDs is that using the mode of topic assignments across the different inference steps is recommended to stabilize the topic assignments, which improves performance. As the inference method is relatively fast in comparison to building a model, this mechanism is a useful and simple improvement, not only restricted to the field of TS. Using more than a single sentence in inference blocks leads to further stability and less sparsity, which improves the results further. In contrast to other TS algorithms using topic models (Misra et al., 2009; Sun et al., 2008), the runtime of TopicTiling is linear in the number of sentences. This makes TopicTiling a fast algorithm with complexity of $O(n)$ (n denoting the number of sentences) as opposed to $O(n^2)$ of the dynamic programming approach as discussed in Fragkou et al. (2004).

Text segmentation benefits from the usage of topic models. As opposed to general-purpose lexical resources, topic models can also find fine-grained subtopical changes, as shown with the segmentation results of the WSJ dataset. Here, most articles have financial content and the topic model can e.g. distinguish between commodity and stock trading. The topic model adapts to the subtopic distribution of the target collection, in contrast e.g. to static WordNet domain labels as in Bentivogli et al. (2004).

For further work, we would like to devise a method to detect the optimal setting for the window parameter w automatically, especially in a setting where the number of target segments is not known in advance. This is an issue that is shared with the original TextTiling algorithm. Moreover, we will extend the usage of our algorithm to more realistic corpora.

Another direction of research that is more generic for approaches based on topic models is the question of how to automatically select appropriate data for topic model estimation, given only a small target collection. Since topic model estimation is computationally expensive, and topic models for generic collections (think Wikipedia) might not suit the needs of a specialized domain (such as with the WSJ data), it is a promising direction to look at target-domain-driven automatic corpus synthesis.

Acknowledgments

This work has been supported by the Hessian research excellence program "Landes-Offensive zur Entwicklung Wissenschaftlich-konomischer Exzellenz" (LOEWE) as part of the research center "Digital Humanities".

References

D. Beeferman, A. Berger, and J. Lafferty. 1999. Statistical models for text segmentation. *Mach. learn.*, 34(1):177–210.

L. Bentivogli, P. Forner, B. Magnini, and E. Pianta. 2004. Revising the wordnet domains hierarchy: semantics, coverage and balancing. In *Proc. COLING 2004 MLR*, pages 101–108, Geneva, Switzerland.

D. M. Blei, A. Y Ng, and M. I. Jordan. 2003. Latent Dirichlet Allocation. *JMLR '03*, 3:993–1022.

F. Y. Y. Choi. 2000. Advances in domain independent linear text segmentation. In *Proc 1st NAACL '00*, pages 26–33, Seattle, WA, USA.

J. Eisenstein. 2009. Hierarchical text segmentation from multi-scale lexical cohesion. In *Proc. NAACL-HLT '09*, pages 353–361, Boulder, CO, USA.

P. Fragkou, V. Petridis, and A. Kehagias. 2004. A Dynamic Programming Algorithm for Linear Text Segmentation. *JIIS '04*, 23(2):179–197.

M. Galley, K. McKeown, E. Fosler-Lussier, and H. Jing. 2003. Discourse segmentation of multi-party conversation. In *Proc 41st ACL '03*, volume 1, pages 562–569, Sapporo, Japan.

T. L. Griffiths and M. Steyvers. 2004. Finding scientific topics. *PNAS*, 101:5228–5235.

M. A. Hearst. 1994. Multi-paragraph segmentation of expository text. In *Proc. 32nd ACL '94*, pages 9–16, Las Cruces, NM, USA.

M. Marcus, G. Kim, M. A. Marcinkiewicz, R. Macintyre, A. Bies, M. Ferguson, K. Katz, and B. Schasberger. 1994. The Penn treebank: Annotating predicate argument structure. In *Proc. ARPA-HLT Workshop '94*, pages 114–119, Plainsboro, NJ, USA.

Hemant Misra, Joemon M Jose, and Olivier Cappé. 2009. Text Segmentation via Topic Modeling : An Analytical Study. In *Proc. 18th CIKM '09*, pages 1553–1556, Hong Kong.

L. Pevzner and M. A. Hearst. 2002. A Critique and Improvement of an Evaluation Metric for Text Segmentation. *Computational Linguistics*, 28.

X.-H. Phan and C.-T. Nguyen. 2007. GibbsLDA++: A C/C++ implementation of latent Dirichlet allocation (LDA). http://jgibblda.sourceforge.net/.

M. Riedl and C. Biemann. 2012a. How text segmentation algorithms gain from topic models. In *Proc. NAACL-HLT '12*, Montreal, Canada.

M. Riedl and C. Biemann. 2012b. Sweeping through the Topic Space: Bad luck? Roll again! In *ROBUS-UNSUP at EACL '12*, Avignon, France.

Q. Sun, R. Li, D. Luo, and X. Wu. 2008. Text segmentation with LDA-based Fisher kernel. In *Proc. 46th ACl-HLT '08*, pages 269–272, Columbus, OH, USA.

M. Utiyama and H. Isahara. 2001. A statistical model for domain-independent text segmentation. In *Proc. 39th ACL '00*, pages 499–506, Toulouse, France.

C. Wayne. 1998. Topic detection and tracking (TDT): Overview & perspective. In *Proc. DARPA BNTUW*, Lansdowne, Virginia.

Y. Yaari. 1997. Segmentation of expository texts by hierarchical agglomerative clustering. In *Proc. RANLP '97*, Tzigov Chark, Bulgaria.

Domain Adaptation of a Dependency Parser with a Class-Class Selectional Preference Model

Raphael Cohen* **Yoav Goldberg**** **Michael Elhadad**
Ben Gurion University of the Negev
Department of Computer Science
POB 653 Be'er Sheva, 84105, Israel
{cohenrap,yoavg,elhadad}@cs.bgu.ac.il

Abstract

When porting parsers to a new domain, many of the errors are related to wrong attachment of out-of-vocabulary words. Since there is no available annotated data to learn the attachment preferences of the target domain words, we attack this problem using a model of selectional preferences based on domain-specific word classes. Our method uses Latent Dirichlet Allocations (LDA) to learn a domain-specific Selectional Preference model in the target domain using un-annotated data. The model provides features that model the affinities among pairs of words in the domain. To incorporate these new features in the parsing model, we adopt the co-training approach and retrain the parser with the selectional preferences features. We apply this method for adapting Easy First, a fast non-directional parser trained on WSJ, to the biomedical domain (Genia Treebank). The Selectional Preference features reduce error by 4.5% over the co-training baseline.

1 Introduction

Dependency parsing captures a useful representation of syntactic structure for information extraction. For example, the Stanford Dependency representation has been used extensively in domain-specific relation extraction tasks such as BioNLP09 (Kim, Ohta et al. 2009) and BioNLP11 (Pyysalo, Ohta et al. 2011). One obstacle to widespread adoption of such syntactic representations is that parsers are generally trained on a specific domain (typically WSJ news data) and it has often been observed that the accuracy of dependency parsers drops significantly when used in a domain other than the training domain.

*Supported by the Lynn and William Frankel Center for Computer Sciences, Ben Gurion University

**Current affiliation: Google Inc.

Domain adaptation for dependency parsing has been explored extensively in the CoNLL 2007 Shared Task (Nivre, Hall et al. 2007). The objective in this task is to adapt an existing parser from a source domain in order to achieve high parsing accuracy on a target domain in which no annotated data is available. Common approaches include self-training (McClosky, Charniak et al. 2006), using word distribution features (Koo, Carreras et al. 2008) and co-training (Sagae and Tsujii 2007) . Dredze *et al.* (Dredze, Blitzer et al. 2007) explored a variety of methods for domain adaptation, which consistently showed little improvement and concluded that domain adaptation for dependency parsing is indeed a hard task. Typically, parsing accuracy drops from 90+% in-domain to 80-84% in the target domain.

When porting parsers to the target domain, many of the errors are related to wrong attachment of out-of-vocabulary words, *i.e.*, words which were not observed when training on the source domain. Since there is not sufficient annotated data to learn the attachment preferences of the target domain words, we attack this problem using a model of selectional preferences based on domain-specific word classes.

Selectional preferences (SP) describe the relative affinity of arguments and head of a syntactic relation. For example, in the sentence: "*D3 activates receptors in blood cells **from** patients*", the preposition "*from*" may be attached to either "*cells*" or "*receptors*". However, the head word "*cells*" has greater affinity to "*patients*" than the candidate "*receptors*" would have towards "*patients*". Note that this preference is highly context-specific.

Several methods for learning SP (not in the context of domain adaptation) have been proposed. Commonly, these methods rely on learning semantic classes for arguments and learning the preference of a predicate to a semantic class. These semantic classes may be derived from manual knowledge bases such as WordNet or FrameNet, or semantic classes learned from large corpora. Recently, Ritter *et* al. (2010) and

Séaghdha (2010) both present induction methods of SP of verb-arguments using LDA (Blei, Ng et al. 2003). Hartung and Frank (2011) extended the LDA-based approach to learning preference for adjective-noun phrases.

In this work, we tackle the task of domain adaptation by developing a domain-specific SP model. Our initial observation is that parsers fail on the target domain when trying to attach domain-specific words not seen during training. We observe as many as 15% of the words are unknown when applying a WSJ-trained parser on Genia and PennBioIE data, compared to only 2.5% in-domain. Parsers trained on the source domain cannot learn attachment preferences for such words. Our motivation is, therefore, to attempt to learn attachment preferences for domain specific words using un-annotated data. Specifically, we focus on acquiring a domain-specific SP model.

Our approach consists of using the low-accuracy source-domain parser on large quantities of in-domain sentences. We extract from the resulting parse trees a collection of syntactically related pairs of words. We then train an LDA model over these pairs of words and derive a domain-specific model of lexical affinities between pairs of words. We finally re-train a parser model to exploit this domain-specific data. To this end, we use the approach of co-training, which consists of identifying reliable parse trees in the target domain in an unsupervised manner using an ensemble of two distinct parsers, and extending the annotated training set with these reliable parse trees. Co-training alone significantly reduces the proportion of unknown words in the re-trained parser – in the extended co-training dataset, we observe that the unknown words rate drops from 15% to 4.5%. Data sparseness, however, remains an issue: 1/3 of the domain-specific words added to the model by co-training appear only once in the extended training set, and we observe that many of the attachment errors are concentrated in a few syntactic configurations (*e.g.,* head(V or N)-prep-pobj, N-N or head(N)-Adj). We extend co-training by introducing our SP model, which is class-based and specific to these difficult syntactic configurations.

Our method reduces error in the Genia Treebank (Tateisi, Yakushiji et al. 2005) by 3.5% over co-training. Introducing additional distributional lexical features (Brown clusters learned in-domain), further reduces error to a total 4.5% reduction. Overall, our parser achieves an accuracy of 83.6% UAS on the Genia domain without annotated data in this domain.

2 Our Approach

To understand the difficulty of domain adaptation, we applied our parser trained on the WSJ news domain to the Genia and measured observed errors. Most of the errors were found in a small set of syntactic configurations: verb-prep-noun, noun-adjective, noun-noun (together these relations make up 32 % of the errors).

For example: in "*nuclear factor-kappa-B DNA-binding activity*" the parser chooses "*factor-kappa-B*" as the head of "*nuclear*" instead of "*activity*". We observe that these errors involve domain-specific vocabulary, and are difficult to disambiguate for non-expert humans as well. Accordingly, we try to acquire a domain-specific model of word-pairs affinities. Our parsing model (EasyFirst) allows us to use such bi-lexical features in an efficient manner. Because of data sparseness, however, we aim to acquire class-based features, and decide to model these lexical preferences using the LDA approach.

Our method proceeds in two stages:

1. Learn selectional preferences from an automatically parsed corpus using LDA on selected syntactic configurations
2. Integrate the preferences into the parsing model as new features using co-training.

2.1 Learning Selectional Preferences

Following (Ritter, Mausam et al. 2010) and (Séaghdha 2010), we model lexical affinity between words in specific syntactic configurations using LDA. Traditionally, LDA learns a set of "topics" from observed documents, based on observed word co-occurrences. In our case, we form artificial documents, which we call syntactic contexts, by collecting head-daughter pairs from parse trees. A syntactic context is constructed for each head word, which contains the related words to which it was found attached.

In the collection process, we identify two syntactic configurations that yield high error rates: *head-prep-noun* and *noun-adj*. We collect two types of syntactic contexts: the preposition contexts contain the set of nouns related to the head through any preposition and the adjective contexts contain the set of adjectives directly related to the head noun. We then learn an LDA model on each of these contexts collections. We use Mallet (McCallum 2002) to learn topic models with hyper-parameter optimization(Wallach, Mimno et al. 2009). The optimal number of topics is selected empirically based on model fit to held-out data.

Source	Relation Type	Semantic Class	Arguments	Predicates
BLLIP	Arg→ Prep → Predicate	Show Business	actors clips soundtrack genre taping characters roles immortalized starred costumes premise screening featured performances poster trumpeted star retrospective clip script	film show movie films movies shows television series stage theater program production version music hollywood broadway
BLLIP	Arg→ Prep → Predicate	Sports	quarterbacks starters pitcher pitchers quarterback coaching receiver linebackers cornerback outfielder baseman fullback	team game league teams games time field players years baseball year rules nfl seasons level player leagues nba club history school state
BLLIP	Arg→ Prep → Predicate	Work Position	jockeying groom groomed relegate relieved unwinding jockeyed selected selecting appointing disqualify named	job post position draft positions candidate team one jobs which role posts successor
Genia	Arg→ Prep → Predicate	Cell-cycle process	stages stage process steps committed block regulator acquire switch points needed directs determinant il-21 proceeds arrest regulators relate d3	differentiation development activation maturation cycle hematopoiesis infection commitment lymphopoiesis stage lineage selection erythropoiesis cascade
Genia	Arg→ Prep → Predicate	Cells and growing conditions	supernatants co-culture co-cultured replication medium surface chemotaxis supernatant beta migration cocultured cultures hyporesponsiveness	cell monocyte lymphocyte pbmc macrophage line blood neutrophil cd dc leukocyte t eosinophil fibroblast platelet keratinocyte
Genia	Adjective→ Noun	Protein activity and regulation	factor-induced tnfalpha-induced agonist-induced thrombin-induced il-2-induced factor-alpha-induced il-1beta-induced cd40-induced rankl-induced augmented il-4-induced	expression activation production phosphorylation response proliferation activity binding secretion apoptosis differentiation translocation release signaling adhesion synthesis generation

Table 1 High affinity classes in the Class-Class Selectional Preferences model extracted with LDA. Classes 1-5 are from preposition head/object pairs (*e.g "groomed for position"* fits the third topic) and class 6 are adjective modifier pairs. Classes 1-3 are from Bllip (un-annotated WSJ corpus) (Charniak, Blaheta et al. 2000) while classes 4-6 are from a corpus composed of Medline abstracts from the Genia (see section 5.1). Class 4 contains arguments and predicates concerning cell-cycle process. In class 5 arguments are cell growing conditions and predicates are types of cells.

The resulting topics represent latent semantic classes of the daughter words. We define a measure of shared affinity between a head word *h* and a candidate daughter word *d* (in a given configuration) s: $Affinty(h,d) = \sum_{c \in Topics} P(c|h) * P(c|d)$ where $P(c|h)$ is the predicted probability of topic *c* given the syntactic context associated to head word *h*. That is, when we apply the LDA model on the syntactic context of *h*, we assign topics to each of the associated daughter words and count their proportion. Note that this affinity measure may predict a non-zero affinity to a pair (*h, d*) even though this word pair has never been observed. The result is a class-class SP model with reduced dimensionality compared to word-word models based for example on PMI. Table 1 lists examples of learned topics. Note that these topics are high-quality semantic clusters that reflect domain semantics, with marked differences between the news and bio-medical domains.

2.2 Co-training to exploit domain features

At this stage, we have acquired a domain-specific model of word affinity that exploits semantic classes and depends on specific syntactic configurations (*head-prep-obj* and *noun-adj*). We now attempt to exploit this model to adapt our source parser to the target domain. To this end, we want to re-train the parser using new features based on the SP model in addition to the original features. We use the framework of co-training to achieve this goal (Sagae and Tsujii 2007): we use two different parsers: Easy-First (Goldberg and Elhadad 2010) and MALT (Nivre, Hall et al. 2006) trained on the same WSJ source domain. We apply these two parsers on a large set of target-domain sentences. We select those sentences where the 2 parsers agree (produce identical trees) and add them to the original source-domain training set. We thus obtain an extended training set with many in-domain samples. We can now re-train the parser using the new SP features.

2.3 SP as features for the Easy First parser

We use the deterministic non-directional Easy-First parser for re-training. This parser incrementally adds edges between words starting with the easier decisions before continuing to difficult ones. Simple structures are first created and their information is available when deciding how to connect complex ones. Easy-First operates in $O(nlogn)$ time compared to $O(n^3)$ of graph-based parsers such as MST (McDonald, Pereira et al. 2005).

As a baseline we use the features provided in the Easy-First distribution. We extend these features with pair-wise affinity measures based on our SP model. The affinity measure ranges from 0 to 1. We bin this measure into (*low, medium, high, very-high*) binary features. When attaching a preposition to its parent, we add one more feature: the affinity of the head candidate with the preposition's daughter (the *pobj*). In addition to these pair-wise features, we also introduce features that correspond to the latent topic class of the words according to each of the 2 acquired LDA models (this introduces one binary feature for each topic). These latent semantic class features are similar in nature to distributional lexical features as used in (Koo, Carreras et al. 2008).

The EasyFirst parser combines partial trees bottom-up. When deciding whether to attach the partial tree "*from patients*" to either "*cells*" or "*receptors*", we compute the affinities of "*cells/patients*" and "*receptors/patients*". Our model produces features indicating *medium* affinity for "*receptors from patients*" and a *high* affinity for *cells from patients*".

3 Experiments and Evaluation

3.1 Genia Treebank

The Genia Treebank (Tateisi, Yakushiji et al. 2005) contains 18K sentences from the biomedical domain, transformed into dependency trees [1] using (De Marneffe, MacCartney et al. 2006)[2]. The corpus contains 2.3K sentences longer than 40 tokens that were excluded from the evaluation. The treebank was divided into test and development sets of equal size.

We created an un-annotated corpus of 200K sentences by querying Medline with the same query terms used to create Genia. We used the Genia POS Tagger on this dataset (Tsuruoka, Tateishi et al. 2005). The corpus was parsed with Easy-First and MALT (arc-eager, polynomial) to create co-training data, yielding 21K sentences with 100% agreement.

The parsed corpus of 200K sentences was used to produce selectional preference models for *adjective-nouns*, with 200 topics, and for *head-prep-object* with 300 topics. We used word lemmas for each pair when preparing syntactic contexts for LDA training (see Table 2).

Relation	# Pairs	# Daughter	# Heads
preposition	360,041	1,727	2,391
adjective	384,347	1,570	2,003

Table 2. Statistics for the training data of the SP model.

3.2 Coverage

Many of the features learned in training a parser are lexicalized; this is an important factor in the drop in accuracy when parsing in a new domain.

To understand the nature of the contribution of the features learned by our SP model, we calculated the coverage of the features acquired in two unsupervised methods: Brown clustering and our SP classes. We count the number of tokens in the Treebank which gain a feature at training time (we ignore punctuation, coordination and preposition tokens). Our SP model covers 53% of the tokens in the test set. Brown clusters calculated with the implementation of Liang (2005) achieve coverage of 73%. Brown clusters features are also class-based distributional features based on n-gram language models, but do not take into account syntactic configurations.

3.3 Adaptation Evaluation

We use a number of baselines for the adaptation task. Three parsers were evaluated on the target domain: Easy-First, MST second order and MALT arc-eager with a polynomial kernel. We report UAS scores of trees of length < 40 without punctuation.

The first baseline setting for each parser is the model trained on WSJ sections 2-21. The second baseline we report is co-training using WSJ 2-21 combined with the 21K full agreement parse trees extracted from Medline, but without new features.

Parser	Training Data	Features	UAS (Exact Match)	
MST	WSJ 2-21		79.6 (10)	
MALT	WSJ 2-21		81.1 (16.6)	
Easy-First	WSJ 2-21		80.5 (12.3)	
MST	Co-Training		81.3 (14.1)	
MALT	Co-Training		82.1 (16.5)	
Easy-First	Co-Training		82.8 (16.2)	
Easy-First	Co-Training	+Brown Clusters	83.1 (17)	+0.3
Easy-First	Co-Training	+SP-Lexicalized	83.0 (16.9)	+0.2
Easy-First	Co-Training	+SP-Lexicalized +SP-Classes	83.4 (16.6)	+0.6
Easy-First	Co-Training	+SP-Lexicalized +SP-Classes +Brown Clusters	**83.6 (17.2)**	+0.8
Easy-First	GeniaTB Dev		89.8 (28.6)	

Table 3. Accuracy for different parser settings on Genia test set. The best performing adapted model trains with co-training data and combines SP and Brown clusters as features.

In Table 3, we see that the combined SP-Features improved the co-training baseline by 0.6%, a significant error reduction of 3.5% (p-value < 0.01).

We list improvement when introducing only pair-wise SP features, and when adding SP-based semantic classes. The effect is also additive with the Brown clusters features, producing an improvement of 0.8% when combined (error reduction of 4.5%).

To evaluate the model adapted for Genia on the general biomedical domain, we used the PennBioIE Treebank . This dataset contains 6K sentences from different biomedical domains. We compared 3 models (see Table 4):

1. Easy-First, MALT and MST trained on WSJ.
2. Easy-First with co-training on Genia.

[1] We use the PTB version of Genia created by Illes Solt.

[2] We convert using the Stanford Parser bundle.

3. Easy-First with co-training on Genia with Selectional Preference features.

Domain adaptation to Genia carried over to the closely related PennBioIE dataset, demonstrating the generalization capability of the method.

Parser	Training Data	Features	UAS	
MALT	WSJ 2-21		78.8	
MST	WSJ 2-21		81.4	
Easy-First	WSJ 2-21		79.8	
Easy-First	Co-Training		81.9	
Easy-First	Co-Training	+SP-Lexicalized +SP-Classes +Brown Clusters	**82.2**	+0.3

Table 4. Accuracy of parsers on PennBioIE Treebank.

3.4 Error Analysis

We compare the parser using the SP pair-wise features for preposition attachment to the co-trained baseline on Genia. The overall accuracy of the parser is improved by 0.2%. However, the two models agree only on 90% of the edges, indicating the new SP features play a very active role when parsing.

For "*E3330 inhibited this induced promoter activity* ***in*** *a dose-dependent manner*", the co-trained parser chose "*activity*" as the head of "*in*" instead of "*inhibited*". The affinity feature in our model for ("*inhibited*", "*manner*") shows affinity of *high* (40-60%) compared to *low* (5-20%) for the wrong pair (*"activity", "manner")*. The same change occurs for "*LysoPC attenuates activation* ***during*** *inflammation and athero-sclerosis*", where the improved model prefers the pair ("*attenuates*", "*inflammation*") to the pair ("*activation*", "*inflammation*") which was chosen by the co-trained model.

The modest overall improvement is due to errors introduced by the new model. In "*Tissue obtained from ectopic pregnancies may identify the mechanism of trophoblast invasion* ***in*** *ectopic pregnancies*", the correct governor of "*in*" is "*invasion*". However, the SP model ranks the affinity of ("*invasion*", "*pregnancies*") lower than that of ("*mechanism*", "*pregnancies*").

Most of the improvement of the full SP model (+0.6%) comes from an improvement in the *N-N* relation from 83% to 84.9% (11% error reduction), this improvement is due to semantic classes features learned on the relations of noun-adjective and head-prep-pobj.

3.5 Effect on NER

Since most of the improvement comes from the N-N relation, we expect improvement for downstream applications such as Named Entity Recognition, a basic task frequently used in the biomedical domain. We use the portion of the Genia Treebank covered by the Genia NER corpus (Kim, Ohta et al. 2004). We expect the inner tokens of a named entity to be connected by relation of N-N or N-Adj. We evaluate the accuracy of these two relations for NE tokens. The Easy-First with co-training baseline produces accuracy of 82.9% on this specific set of relations, improved by the SP model to 84.4%, a reduction in error of 8.7%.

4 Related Work

4.1 Learning of Selectional Preference

Preference of predicate-argument pairs has been studied in depth with a number of approaches. Resnik (1993) suggested a class-based model for preference of predicates combining WordNet classes with mutual information techniques for associating an argument with a predicate class from WordNet.

Another approach models words in a corpus as context vectors (Erk and Pado 2008; Turney and Pantel 2010) for discovering predicate or argument classes using large corpora or the Web.

Recently, semantic classes were successfully induced using LDA topic modeling. These methods have shown success in modeling verb argument relationship to a single predicate (Ritter, Mausam et al. 2010) or a predicate pair (Séaghdha 2010), as well as for adjective-noun preference (Hartung and Frank 2011).

4.2 Learning SP for improving dependency parsing

The argument-predicate choice learned in SP is directly related to the decision of creating an edge between them in a parse tree. Van Noord (2007) modeled verb-noun preferences using pointwise mutual information (PMI) using an automatically parsed corpus in Dutch. Association scores of pairs were added as features improving the accuracy significantly from 87.4% to 87.9%.

Nakov and Hearst (Nakov and Hearst 2005) focused on resolving PP attachments and coordination. They used co-occurrence counts from web queries in order to estimate selectional restrictions.

Zhou *et al.* (2011) used N-gram counts from Google search and Google V1 to deduce word-word attachment preferences. They used these counts in a pair-wise mutual information (PMI) scheme as features for improving parsing in the News domain (WSJ) and adaptation for biomedical domain. Their evaluation showed improvement of 1% on WSJ section 23 over the vanilla MST parser and a significant increase in the domain adaptation problem.

4.3 Domain adaptation of dependency parsing

Domain adaptation for dependency parsing has been studied mostly in regard to the CoNLL 2007 shared task (Nivre, Hall et al. 2007). Both of the leading methods included learning from a parser ensemble. Attardi *et al.*'s (2007) used a weak parser in order to identify common parsing errors and overcome those in the training of a stronger parser. Sagae and Tsujii (2007) used two different parsers to parse un-annotated in-domain data and used the trees where the two parsers agreed to augment the training corpus.

Dredze *et al.* (2007) approached the "closed" problem, *i.e.*, without using additional un-annotated data. They used the PennBioIE Treebank and applied a number of adaptation techniques: (1) features concerning NPs such as chunking information and frequency; (2) word distribution features; (3) features encoding information from diverse parsers; (4) target focused learning – giving greater weight in training to sentences which are more likely in a target domain language model. These methods have not improved accuracy over the baseline of the MST parser (McDonald, Pereira et al. 2005) trained on WSJ.

5 Conclusion

Learning class-class selectional preferences from a large in-domain corpus assists dependency parsing significantly. We have suggested a method for learning selectional preference classes for a specific domain using an existing parser and a standard implementation of LDA topic modeling. The SP model can be used for estimating the affinity between a pair of tokens or simply as a feature of semantic class association. This approach is faster when querying the model for the affinity of a pair of words than a PMI model suggested by Zhou *et al.*(2011). While covering fewer tokens in the target test set than Brown clusters, the method achieved a higher improvement of parsing performance. Furthermore, some of the improvement was additive and reduced UAS error by 4.5% compared to a strong co-training baseline.

6 References

Attardi, G., F. Dell'Orletta, et al. (2007). Multilingual dependency parsing and domain adaptation using DeSR. ACL.

Blei, D. M., A. Y. Ng, et al. (2003). "Latent dirichlet allocation." JMLR **3**: 993-1022.

Charniak, E., D. Blaheta, et al. (2000). "Bllip 1987-89 wsj corpus release 1." LDC.

De Marneffe, M. C., B. MacCartney, et al. (2006). Generating typed dependency parses from phrase structure parses. LREC.

Dredze, M., J. Blitzer, et al. (2007). Frustratingly hard domain adaptation for dependency parsing. CoNLL 2007.

Erk, K. and S. Pado (2008). A structured vector space model for word meaning in context. EMNLP 2008**:** 897-906.

Goldberg, Y. and M. Elhadad (2010). An efficient algorithm for easy-first non-directional dependency parsing. NAACL 2010**:** 742-750.

Hartung, M. and A. Frank (2011). Exploring Supervised LDA Models for Assigning Attributes to Adjective-Noun Phrases. ACL.

Kim, J.-D., T. Ohta, et al. (2009). Overview of BioNLP'09 shared task on event extraction. Current Trends in Biomedical NLP, ACL**:** 1-9.

Kim, J.-D., T. Ohta, et al. (2004). Introduction to the bio-entity recognition task at JNLPBA. Proceedings of the International Joint Workshop on Natural Language Processing in Biomedicine and its Applications. Geneva, Switzerland, Association for Computational Linguistics**:** 70-75.

Koo, T., X. Carreras, et al. (2008). Simple semi-supervised dependency parsing. ACL 2008**:** 595-603.

Liang, P. (2005). Semi-supervised learning for natural language, Massachusetts Institute of Technology.

McCallum, A. K. (2002). "Mallet: A machine learning for language toolkit."

McClosky, D., E. Charniak, et al. (2006). Effective self-training for parsing, ACL.

McDonald, R., F. Pereira, et al. (2005). Non-projective dependency parsing using spanning tree algorithms. EMNLP**:** 523-530.

Nakov, P. and M. Hearst (2005). Using the web as an implicit training set: application to structural ambiguity resolution. EMNLP, Association for Computational Linguistics**:** 835-842.

Nivre, J., J. Hall, et al. (2007). The CoNLL 2007 Shared Task on Dependency Parsing, CoNLL 2007. **s. 915-932**.

Nivre, J., J. Hall, et al. (2006). Maltparser: A data-driven parser-generator for dependency parsing.

Noord, G. v. (2007). Using self-trained bilexical preferences to improve disambiguation accuracy. 10th International Conference on Parsing Technologies, ACL**:** 1-10.

Pyysalo, S., T. Ohta, et al. (2011). "Overview of the Entity Relations (REL) supporting task of BioNLP 2011." ACL HLT 2011 **1**(480): 83.

Ritter, A., Mausam, et al. (2010). A latent dirichlet allocation method for selectional preferences. ACL 2010**:** 424-434.

Sagae, K. and J.-i. Tsujii (2007). Dependency parsing and domain adaptation with LR models and parser ensembles. EMNLP-CoNLL 2007**:** 1044-1050.

Séaghdha, D. (2010). Latent variable models of selectional preference. ACL 2010**:** 435-444.

Tateisi, Y., A. Yakushiji, et al. (2005). Syntax Annotation for the GENIA corpus. ACL.

Tsuruoka, Y., Y. Tateishi, et al. (2005). "Developing a robust part-of-speech tagger for biomedical text." AII: 382-392.

Turney, P. D. and P. Pantel (2010). "From frequency to meaning: Vector space models of semantics." JAIR **37**(1): 141-188.

Wallach, H., D. Mimno, et al. (2009). "Rethinking LDA: Why priors matter." NIPS **22**: 1973–1981.

Zhou, G., J. Zhao, et al. (2011). Exploiting web-derived selectional preference to improve statistical dependency parsing. ACL.

Extracting fine-grained durations for verbs from Twitter

Jennifer Williams
Department of Linguistics
Georgetown University
Washington, DC USA
jaw97@georgetown.edu

Abstract

This paper presents recent work on a new method to automatically extract fine-grained duration information for common verbs using a large corpus of Twitter tweets. Regular expressions were used to extract verbs and durations from each tweet in a corpus of more than 14 million tweets with 90.38% precision covering 486 verb lemmas. Descriptive statistics for each verb lemma were found as well as the most typical fine-grained duration measure. Mean durations were compared with previous work by Gusev et al. (2011) and it was found that there is a small positive correlation.

1 Introduction

Implicit information about events is crucial to any natural language processing task involving temporal understanding and reasoning. This information comes in many forms, among them knowledge about typical durations for events and knowledge about typical times at which an event occurs. We know that lunch lasts for perhaps an hour and takes place around noon, and so when we interpret a text such as "After they ate lunch, they played a game of chess and then went to the zoo" we can infer that the chess game probably lasted for a few hours and not for several months.

This paper describes a new method for extracting information about typical durations for verbs from tweets posted to the Twitter microblogging site. Twitter is a rich resource for information about everyday events – people post their 'tweets' to Twitter publicly in real-time as they conduct their activities throughout the day, resulting in a significant amount of information about common events. Data from Twitter is more diverse than the data found in news articles that has typically been used for looking at event durations (Pan et al., 2011). For example, consider that (1) was used find out that working can last for an hour and a half:

(1) *Had work for an hour and 30 mins now going to disneyland with my cousins :)*

I extracted and analyzed a large number of such tweets containing temporal duration information. This involved identifying relevant tweets, extracting the temporal phrases, and associating these with the verb they modified. The processes are described below. Two objectives were investigated in this paper: (1) how to automatically extract duration information for common verbs from Twitter, and (2) to discover the duration distributions for common verbs. A wide range of factors influence typical durations. Among these are the character of a verb's arguments, the presence of negation and other embedding features. For example, *eating a snack* is different from *eating a meal* since these events have different durations. To simplify the task, I set aside tweets wherein the sentence-level verb was negated, or in the conditional or future tenses. Examining the effect of verb arguments was also set aside in this work.

The problem of finding typical duration for events can be viewed as a coarse-grained task or a fine-grained task. At the coarse-grained level it could be determined whether or not a chess game lasts for more or less than one day, whereas a fine-grained analysis would indicate that a chess game lasts for minutes or hours.

The results of this work show that Twitter can be mined for duration information with high accuracy using regular expressions. Likewise, the typical durations for verbs can be summarized in terms of the most frequent duration-measure (seconds, minutes, hours, days, weeks, months, years, decades) as well as by descriptive statistics.

2 Prior Work

Past research on typical durations has made use of standard corpora with texts from literature excerpts, news stories, and full-length weblogs (Pan et al., 2011; Kozareva & Hovy, 2011; Gusev et al., 2011). However, data from Twitter has been useful for other NLP tasks such as detecting sarcasm (González-Ibáñez et al., 2011), as well as sentiment for Twitter events (Thelwall et al., 2011). The present work used data from Twitter because it is readily available and diverse in its linguistic nature.

2.1 Hand-Annotation

The first to examine typical durations of events was Pan et al. (2011). They describe a method to annotate events with duration information. They hand-annotated a portion of the TIMEBANK corpus that consisted of news articles and non-financial articles from the Wall Street Journal. They did this for 48 news articles (for 2,132 events) and 10 Wall Street Journal articles (for 156 events). For each event, three annotators indicated a lower-bound duration and an upper-bound duration that would cover 80% of the possible cases provided that durations are normally distributed. They converted the upper and lower bounds into distributions. They defined annotator agreement to be the average overlap of all the pairwise overlapping areas, calculated using the kappa statistic.

In their experiments, Pan et al. (2011) examined their annotation guidelines and found that annotator agreement was significantly improved after annotators were instructed to use their guidelines. These guidelines took into consideration information about event classes. The final guidelines addressed the following kinds of classes: actions vs. states, aspectual events, reporting events (quoted and unquoted reporting), multiple events, events involving negation, appearance events, and positive infinitive duration[1]. Human agreement for coarse-grained analysis was reported to be 87.7% whereas agreement for fine-grained analysis was 79.8%.

Hand-annotation is an expensive way of acquiring typical duration and human annotators do not always agree on how long events last. This paper presents a way to extract duration information automatically and at a fine-grained scale to discover the kinds of distributions of durations for different verbs as well as their typical durations.

2.2 Web Extraction

To compile temporal duration information for a wider range of verbs, Gusev et al. (2011) explored a Web-based query method for harvesting typical durations of events. They used five different kinds of query frames to extract events and their durations from the web at a coarse-grained level and at a fine-grained level. They compiled a lexicon of 10,000 events and their duration distributions.

In the work of Gusev et al. (2011), they calculated the most likely duration for events at a fine-grained scale. To obtain each of the fine-grained duration distributions, they first binned durations into their temporal unit measures (seconds, minutes, hours, etc.). Next, they discarded data that was extracted using patterns that had very low “hit-counts” in their effort to judge the reliability of their extraction frames. Finally, they normalized the distributions based on how often each pattern occurs in general. They note that many verbs have a two-peaked distribution. When used with a duration marker, *run*, for example, is used about 15% of the time with hour-scale and 38% with year-scale duration markers. In the case of the event *say*, Gusev et al. (2011) chose to normalize their duration distributions with a heuristic to account for the possibility that all of the year-scale durations could

[1] Positive infinitive durations describe states that will last forever once they begin, such as being dead.

be attributed to the common phrase "... for years".

Kozareva and Hovy (2011) also collected typical durations of events using Web query patterns. They proposed a six-way classification of ways in which events are related to time, but provided only programmatic analyses of a few verbs using Web-based query patterns. They have asked for a compilation of the 5,000 most common verbs along with their typical temporal durations. In each of these efforts, automatically collecting a large amount of reliable data which covers a wide range of verbs has been noted as a difficulty.

3 Methodology

3.1 Data Collection

For the present study, tweets were collected from the Twitter web service API using an open-source Python module called Tweetstream (Halvorsen & Schierkolk, 2010)[2]. Specifically, tweets were collected that contained reference to a temporal duration. The data collection task began on February 1, 2011 and ended on September 28, 2011. The total number of tweets in the collected corpus was 14,801,607 and the total number of words in the corpus was 224,623,447.

The following query terms (denoting temporal duration measure) were used to extract tweets containing temporal duration from the Twitter stream:

second, seconds, minute, minutes, hour, hours, day, days, week, weeks, month, months, year, years, decade, decades, century, centuries, sec, secs, min, mins, hr, hrs, wk, wks, yr, yrs

Tweets were normalized, tokenized, and then tagged for POS, using the NLTK Treebank Tagger (Bird & Loper, 2004). Each tweet came with a unique tweet ID number provided by Twitter and this ID was used to inform whether or not there were duplicate entries in the dataset, and all duplicate entries were removed. The twitter stream was also filtered so that it did not include re-tweets (tweets that have been reposted to Twitter).

3.2 Extraction Frames

To associate a temporal duration with each verb, the verbs and durations were matched and extracted using four types of regular expression extraction frames. The patterns applied a heuristic to associate each verb with a temporal expression, similar to the extraction frames used by Gusev et al. (2011). Unlike Gusev et al. (2011) four different extraction frames were used (*for, in, spend*, and *take*) with varied tense and aspect on each frame, in an effort to widen the coverage of extractions compared with that of Gusev et al. (2011). Each of the four frames were associated with a set of regular expressions to match and extract verbs for two tenses (past and present), and three different aspects (simple, perfect, and progressive). Durations could match spelled out numbers (one hour), hyphenated numbers (twenty-one minutes), or digits (30 minutes).

FOR: The for-adverbial extraction frame was designed to match two tenses and three aspects. The regular expressions accounted for variation in the word ordering. Consider some simplified pattern examples below, which show varied word order and tense-aspect combinations:

- *John ran for 10 minutes*
- *for ten minutes Sally was running*

IN: The in-adverbial extraction frame is tricky for extracting durations because the in-adverbial is sometimes used to describe pending events or things that are about to happen, such as, "Sally is going to the store in 5 minutes". However, I wanted to avoid collecting durations for future events. Therefore any verbs that matched the in-adverbial extraction frame were restricted to match the perfect aspect with any tense or the past tense and with any aspect, to indicate that a given event has been completed.

SPEND/TAKE: The tense and aspect were not restricted and the tweets were matched for tense and aspect on *spend* and *take*. In these cases the durations were syntactically associated with spend and take whereas semantically, the durations were associated with the verb in the complement clause (*read, work*, etc.). Variations in word order, like that found in examples of the *for* extraction frame, were not allowed for tweets matching the *spend* extraction frame. We see in the examples below that the verb is *read* and the tense and aspect in each of the examples were found to be past progressive:

- *Susie was spending 30 minutes reading*

[2] This Python module is available open-source at: https://bitbucket.org/runeh/tweetstream/src/

- *Susie was taking 5 minutes to read it*

3.3 Post-Processing Extracted Tweets

There were several steps to the post-processing of tweets. First, I identified the verb lemmas using NLTK WordNet (Bird and Loper, 2004). Verb lemmas that occurred less than 100 times were removed.

Next, all of the durations-measures were converted into seconds using a separate set of regular expressions. Instances where the duration lasted for longer than 1 billion seconds were removed. There were 6,389 tweets that met this condition. These tweets were removed in an attempt to avoid figurative speech that can occur on Twitter. So tweets such as the ones shown in (2) and (3) were removed:

(2) *I hate when I order food and it takes 2009779732 years to come*

(3) *I think my iTunes library is too big, it takes 7987694564 years to open*

Not all of the temporal durations that were extracted were numerically measured. Tweets that contained indefinite determiners *a* or *an* were treated as having a value of 1 temporal unit so that the noun phrase "an hour" could be converted to *3600 seconds*. There were 51,806 such tweets. Some of the tweets contained expressions such as: "some hours", "many hours", and "several hours". In cases like these, the duration was treated as having a value of based on its temporal unit so that durations like "many hours" were treated as *one hour*. This was applied to all of the temporal durations that were not numerically measured[3].

In addition, tweets that matched more than one extraction frame were removed. After the post-processing stage 390,562 tweets were extracted that covered 486 verb lemmas.

3.4 Extraction Frame Evaluation

Extraction frame precision was estimated for each frame by hand-annotating a randomly selected sample and labeling each extracted tweet as relevant if the duration, tense, aspect and verb were identified. The extraction frames performed overall with 90.38% precision, estimated from a sample size determined by the two-tailed t-test for proportions with 95% confidence (n=400, p=0.05).

[3]There were 35,553 tweets matching this criteria.

The extraction frame precision is reported below in Table 1.

Extraction Frame Type	**Estimated Precision**	**# Tweets**
for	91.25%	270,624
in	72.25%	83,061
spend	99.75%	2,593
take	98.25%	34,284
Overall	90.38%	390,562

Table 1. Number of extracted tweets

4 Analysis of Durations

4.1 Duration Distributions

Twitter is a lucrative resource for gathering typical durations associated with common verbs at a fine-grained level. Some verbs were found to have a very short mean duration (consider *rain* and *snooze*) while some had a longer mean duration (consider *live* and *work*), shown in Table 2.

Short durations		**Long durations**	
doze	32,721	*grow*	197,921,586
jog	405,550	*smoke*	246,557,468
cough	4,756,427	*live*	247,274,960
rain	4,994,776	*marry*	312,000,000
meet	40,503,127	*exist*	341,174,881

Table 2. Mean durations (in seconds) for a sample of verb lemmas

The following plots (Figures 1-3) show the frequency distribution for three different lemmas: *wrestle, say,* and *boil*. Similar to the work done by Pan et al. (2011) and Gusev et al. (2011), this research also shows that some of the duration distributions are bimodal. Gusev et al. (2011), Pan et al. (2011), and recent work by Williams and Katz (2012) show that some bimodal distributions could be associated with iterative events or habituality.

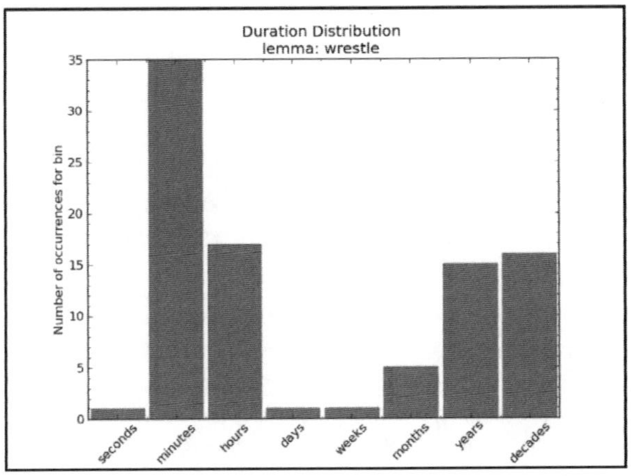

Figure 1. Distribution for *wrestle*, typically takes minutes or years

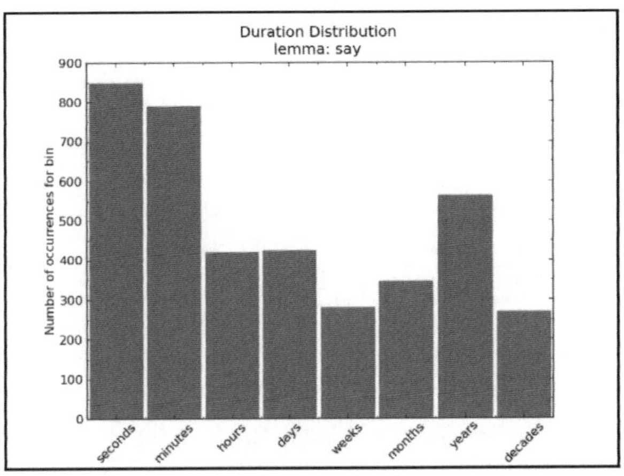

Figure 2. Distribution for *say*, typically takes seconds or years

The bimodal distributions for *wrestle* and *say* could possibly indicate that there are two phenomena present in the distributions: durations for events, and durations for habits. Consider that the sentence "John wrestled for half and hour with his kids" describes an event whereas the sentence "John wrestled for 30 years as a pro" describes a habit. An analysis of the relationship between bimodal distributions and habituality would provide more information in future work.

Not all of the distributions are bimodal, in fact we can see that is the case with the distribution for *boil*. Users of Twitter are not usually reporting long durations for that verb, but they do in several rare cases. This could be due to the effects of figurative speech, as in "John has been making by blood boil for decades".

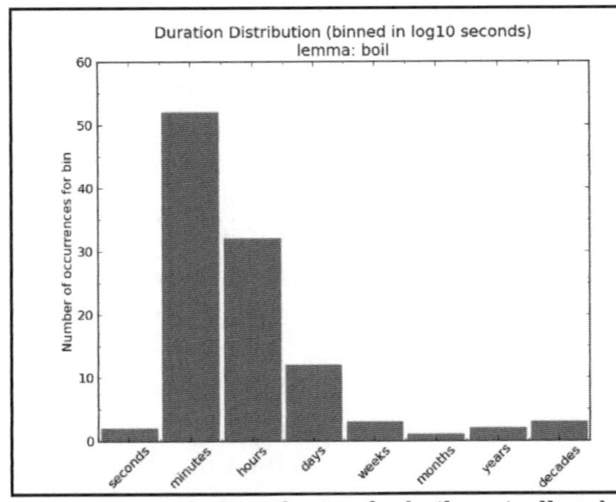

Figure 3. Distribution for boil, typically takes minutes

4.2 Comparison of Previous Work

To compare my work with Gusev et al., (2011), I found the overlap of verb lemmas. There were 356 verb lemmas in common. I calculated the $\log_{10}$ of each mean duration associated with each verb lemma, for my data and theirs. I plotted my means versus their means and I used linear regression to find a best fit line. The Pearson correlation value was 0.46 ($p < 0.01$), which suggests a weak positive correlation. Some of the outliers that we see in Figure 4 correspond to the following verb lemmas: *freeze, judge, age, double, load, lock, revise, score, heat, remove, lose, meet, head, ring, skate, yell,* and *fall.*

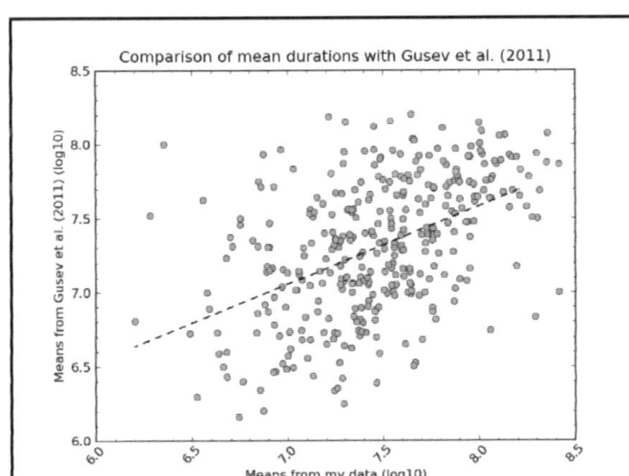

Figure 4. Mean durations vs. Gusev et al. (2011) in $\log_{10}$ seconds

5 Discussion

This paper has presented a new method to automatically extract duration information for verbs using data from Twitter. The four extraction frames used here were 90.25% accurate. This indicates that regular expressions can be applied to tweets to associate an event with its duration. Comparison with previous work shows that there is a positive correlation, and this indicates that the method presented here is nearly comparable. Corpora, extracted tweets, durations, and other materials used in this study will be made publicly available at the following website:

https://sites.google.com/site/relinguistics/

6 Future Work

There were several aspects of natural language that were put aside in this research. Future work should compare how the duration distributions are affected by modality, negation, and the future tense/aspect combinations. And, although I briefly addressed the presence of figurative language, this work could benefit from knowing which tweets were figurative, since this may affect how we examine typical durations.

Only four types of extraction frames were used in this study. More work is needed to find out if there are other extraction frames that can be used for this same task, and exactly which extraction frames should be used under various circumstances. Future work could also address the combinatorial effects of modality, negation, future tenses, and verb arguments with typical duration. Events like "John might finish writing his email soon" and "John might finish writing his memoir soon" will have different kinds of durations associated with them.

Looking at the distributions presented here, it is not clear where the boundary might be between single episodes, iterative events or habits. This kind of distinction between habits and events could prove to be important because an event such as *exist* can go on for years, decades or centuries, and in some cases *exist* might only last for a few seconds – but we would not say that *exist* is a habit. At the same time, the frequency distribution for *wrestle* in Figure 1 indicates that the event *wrestle* lasts for hours, but the fact that it is reported to last for years suggests that there are some habits in the collected data.

References

Steven Bird and Edward Loper. 2004. NLTK: The natural language toolkit. In *Proceedings of 42nd Annual Meeting of the Association for Computational Linguistics (ACL-04).*

Roberto González-Ibáñez, Smaranda Muresan, and Nina Wacholder. 2011. "Identifying sarcasm in Twitter: a closer look". In *Proceedings of the 49th Annual Meeting of the Association for Computational Linguistics* (pp. 581–586), Portland, Oregon, June 19-24.

Andrey Gusev, Nathaniel Chambers, Pranav Khaitan, Divye Khilnani, Steven Bethard, and Dan Jurafsky. 2011. "Using query patterns to learn the durations of events". *IEEE IWCS-2011, 9th International Conference on Web Services.* Oxford, UK 2011.

Rune Halvorsen, and Christopher Schierkolk. 2010. Tweetstream: Simple Twitter Streaming API (Version 0.3.5) [Software]. Available from https://bitbucket.org/runeh/tweetstream/src/

Jerry Hobbs and James Pustejovsky. 2003. "Annotating and reasoning about time and events". In *Proceedings of the AAAI Spring Symposium on Logical Formulation of Commonsense Reasoning*. Stanford University, CA 2003.

Zornitsa Kozareva and Eduard Hovy. 2011. "Learning Temporal Information for States and Events". In *Proceedings of the Workshop on Semantic Annotation for Computational Linguistic Resources (ICSC 2011)*, Stanford.

Marc Moens and Mark Steedman. 1988. "Temporal Ontology and Temporal Reference". *Computational Linguistics* 14(2):15-28.

Feng Pan, Rutu Mulkar-Mehta, and Jerry R. Hobbs. 2011. "Annotating and Learning Event Durations in Text." *Computational Linguistics*. 37(4):727-752.

Mike Thelwall, Kevan Buckley, and Georgios Paltoglou. 2011. "Sentiment in Twitter events." *Journal of the American Society of Information Science and Technology*, 62: 406–418. doi: 10.1002/asi.21462

Jennifer Williams and Graham Katz. 2012. "Extracting and modeling durations for habits and events from Twitter". In *Proceedings of Association for Computational Linguistics, ACL 2012*. Jeju, Republic of Korea.

Discourse Structure in Simultaneous Spoken Turkish

Işın Demirşahin
Middle East Technical University
Informatics Institute, Cognitive Science
ODTU, 06800, Ankara, TURKEY
disin@metu.edu.tr

Abstract

The current debate regarding the data structure necessary to represent discourse structure, specifically whether tree-structure is sufficient to represent discourse structure or not, is mainly focused on written text. This paper reviews some of the major claims about the structure in discourse and proposes an investigation of discourse structure for simultaneous spoken Turkish by focusing on tree-violations and exploring ways to explain them away by non-structural means.

1 Introduction

There is an ongoing debate about the nature of structure in discourse. Halliday and Hasan (1976) propose that although there is some structure in the text and structure implies *texture;* texture does not necessarily imply structure. Text is held together by a variety of non-structural cohesive ties: *reference, substitution, ellipsis, conjunction* and *lexical cohesion.* However, their notion of structure is strictly syntactic; and for other researchers, the elements that hold the text together, especially elements of conjunction, can be taken as indicators of structure in discourse.

If there is structure in discourse, the complexity of the said structure is of interest to linguistics, cognitive science and computer science alike. Is discourse structure more complex or more simple than that of sentence level syntax? How and to what degree is that structure constrained? In order to answer questions along these lines, researchers explore the possible data structures for discourse in natural language resources.

Section 2, reviews the current approaches to discourse structure. Section 3 introduces the current study, i.e., the search for deviations from tree structure in spontaneous spoken language. Section 4 presents a conclusive summary.

2 The Structure of Discourse

2.1 Tree Structure for Discourse

Hobbs (1985) takes it as a fact that discourse has structure. He argues that a set of coherence relations build a discourse structure that is composed of trees of successive and sometimes intertwining trees of various sizes connected at the peripheries.

Rhetorical Structure Theory (RST) (Mann and Thompson, 1988) proposes that a text can be analyzed as a single tree structure by means of predefined rhetorical relations. Rhetorical relations hold between adjacent constituents either asymmetrically between a *nucleus* and a *satellite*, or symmetrically between two nuclei. The notion of *nuclearity* allows the units to connect to previous smaller units that are already embedded in a larger tree structure, because a relation is assumed to be shared by the nuclei of non-atomic constituents. In other words, a relation to a complex discourse unit can be interpreted as either between the adjacent unit and the whole of the complex unit, or between the adjacent unit and a nucleus of the complex unit.

One of the rhetorical structures in RST, *elaboration* is criticized by Knott et al. (2001) who propose an elaboration-less coherence structure, where the global focus defines linearly organized *entity chains,* which can contain multiple atomic or non-atomic RS trees, and which are linked via non-rhetorical resumptions.

Discourse - Lexicalized Tree Adjoining Grammar (D-LTAG) (Webber, 2004) is an extension of the sentence-level Tree Adjoining Grammar (Joshi, 1987) to discourse level. Discourse connectives act as discourse level predicates that connect two spans of text with abstract object (Asher, 1993) interpretations. Coordinating and subordinating conjunctions such as *fakat* 'but' (1) and *rağmen* 'although' (2), take their host clauses by substitution and the other argument either by substitution or by adjoining; whereas discourse adverbials such as (3) take the host argument by adjoining, and the other argument anaphorically. In the examples below, the host argument is in boldface, the other argument is in italics and the connectives are underlined.

(1) *Araştırma Merkezi aşağı yukarı bitmiş durumda*, fakat **iç ve dış donanımı eksik.**

'The Research Center is more or less complete but **its internal and external equipments are missing.'**

(2) **Benim için çok utandırıcı bir durum olmasına** rağmen *oralı olmuyordum.*

'Although **it was a very embarrassing situation for me**, *I didn't pay much heed.'*

(3) İlgisizliğim seni şaşırtabilir. ama *üvey babamı görmek istemediğim için yıllardır o eve gitmiyorum.* ***Anneme çok bağlı olduğumu da söyleyemem*** *ayrıca.*

My indifference might surprise you, but *since I do not want to see my stepfather, I have not been to that house for years.* In addition, **I cannot say I am attached to my mom much.**

As in sentence level syntax, the anaphoric relations are not part of the structure; as a result, the discourse adverbials can access their first arguments anywhere in the text without violating non-crossing constraint of tree structure. When a structural connective such as *ve* 'and' and a discourse adverbial such as *bundan* ötürü 'therefore' are used together as in (4), an argument may have multiple parents violating one of the constraints of the tree structure; but since the discourse adverbial takes the other argument anaphorically, the non-crossing constraint is not violated.

(4) *Dedektif romanı içinden çıkılmaz gibi görünen esrarlı bir cinayetin çözümünü sunduğu için, her şeyden önce mantığa güveni ve inancı dile getiren bir anlatı türüdür* ve bundan ötürü de **burjuva rasyonelliğinin edebiyattaki özü haline gelmiştir.**

Unraveling the solution to a seemingly intricate murder mystery, the detective novel is a narrative genre which primarily gives voice to the faith and trust in reason and being so, **it has become the epitome of bourgeois rationality in the literature.**

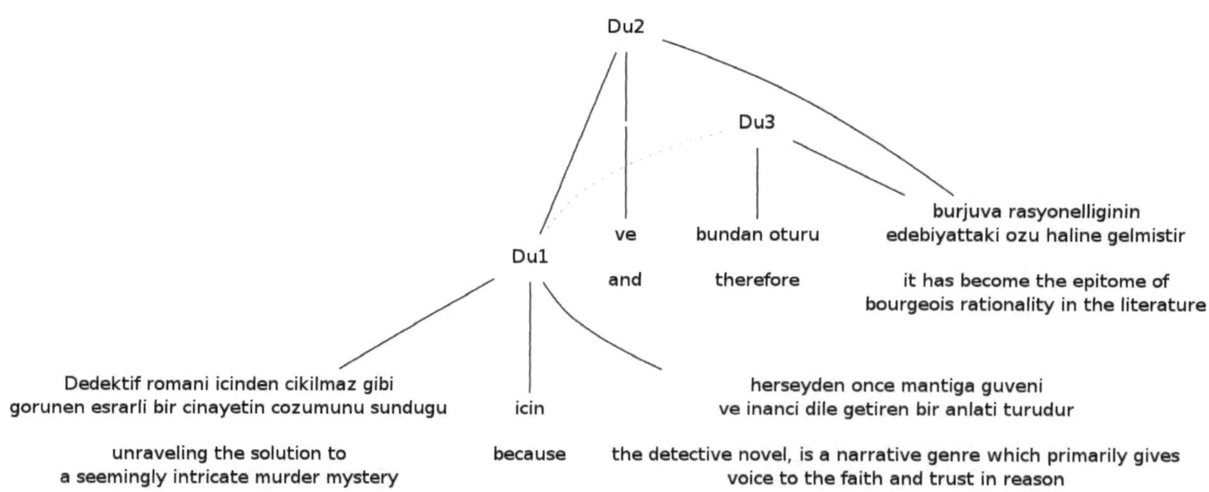

Figure 1: Tree structure for (4). *Bundan ötürü* 'therefore' takes one argument anaphorically, shown as a dotted line in this representation. Since the anaphora is non structural, there is no crossing in (4). However, tree structure is still violated because Du2 and Du3 share an argument, resulting in multiple-parent structure.

Implicit connectives always link two adjacent spans structurally, the host span by substitution and the other by adjoining. Since after adjunction the initial immediate dominance configurations are not preserved, the semantic composition is defined on the derivation tree rather than the derived tree (Forbes et al., 2003; Forbes-Riley et al., 2005).

The Penn Discourse Treebank (PDTB) (Prasad et al., 2008) is loosely based on D-LTAG, as the discourse connectives are annotated as discourse level predicates with two arguments; but the focus is no longer on the global structure of discourse but on individual relations, and the annotations are kept as theory-neutral as possible.

2.2 Deviations from Tree Structure

Wolf and Gibson (2005), judging from a corpus annotated for a set of relations that is based on Hobbs (1985), argue that the global discourse structure cannot be represented by a tree structure. They point out that the definition for the anaphoric connectives in D-LTAG seems to be circular, since they are defined by their anaphoric arguments which can be involved in crossing dependencies, and in turn they are defined as anaphoric and thus outside the structural constraints. They propose a chain graph-based annotations scheme, which they claim express the discourse relations more accurately than RST, because the relations can access embedded, non-nuclear constituents that would be inaccessible in an RST tree.

Since Wolf and Gibson use attribution and same relations, which are not considered discourse relations in D-LTAG or the PDTB, a direct comparison of chain graph annotations and the PDTB does not seem possible at this point; but violations of tree structure are also attested in the PDTB.

Lee et al. (2006, 2008) investigate the PDTB and identify dependencies that are compatible with tree structure, *independent relations* and *full embedding*; as well as incompatible dependencies, *shared argument, properly contained argument, partially overlapping arguments,* and *pure crossing*. They claim that only shared arguments (same text span taken as argument by two distinct discourse connectives) and properly contained arguments (a text span that is the argument of one connective properly contains a smaller text span that is the argument of another connective) should be considered as contributing to the complexity of discourse structure; the reason being that the instances of partially overlapping arguments and pure crossing can be explained away by anaphora and attribution, both of which are non-structural phenomena. The presence of shared arguments carries the discourse structure from tree to directed acyclic graphs (Webber et al., 2011).

Aktaş et al. (2010) have identified similar tree structure violations in the Turkish Discourse Bank (TDB) (Zeyrek et al., 2010). In addition to the dependencies in Lee et al. (2006), Aktaş have identified *properly contained relations* and *nested relations*. A full analysis of the TDB with respect to discourse structure is yet to be done.

Egg and Redeker (2008, 2010) argue that tree structure violations can be overcome by applying an underspecification formalism to discourse representation. They adopt a weak interpretation of *nuclearity*, where although the relation between an atomic constituent and a complex constituent is understood to hold between the atomic constituent ant the *nucleus* of the complex constituent, structurally the relation does not access the nucleus of the complex, and therefore does not result in multiple parenting. This approach is not directly applicable to PDTB-style relations, because of the *minimality principle*, which constrains the annotators to select the smallest text span possible that is necessary to interpret the discourse relation when annotating the arguments of a discourse connective.

Egg and Redeker also argue that most of the crossing dependencies in Wolf and Gibson (2005) involve anaphora, which is considered non-structural in discourse as well as in syntax. However, they admit that *multi-satellite constructions* (MSC) in RST, where one constituent can enter into multiple rhetorical relations as long as it is the nucleus of all relations, seems to violate tree structure. They state that only some of the MSCs can be expressed as atomic-to-complex relations, but they also state that those the MSCs that cannot be expressed so seems to be genre specific. The fact that both Egg and Redeker (2008) and Lee et al. (2006, 2008) cannot refute the presence of multiple parenting in discourse structure is striking.

2.3 Discourse Structure in Spoken Language

All studies in Section 2 investigates discourse structure in written texts. There are spoken corpora annotated for RST such as Stent (2000) and SDRT

(Baldridge & Lascarides, 2005), but the only PDTB-style spoken discourse structure annotation within the author's knowledge is part of the LUNA corpus in Italian (Tonelli, 2010).

The most striking change Tonelli et al. made in the PDTB annotation scheme when annotating spoken dialogues is to allow for implicit relations between non-adjacent text spans due to higher fragmentation in spoken language. They also added an *interruption* label for when a single argument of a speaker was interrupted. Some changes to the PDTB Sense Hierarchy was necessary including the addition of the GOAL type under CONTINGENCY class, fine tuning of PRAGMATIC subtypes, exclusion of LIST type from EXPANSION class and merging of syntactically distinguished REASON and RESULT subtypes into a semantically defined CAUSE type.

3 Proposed Study and Methodology

The aim of the current study is to determine whether tree structure is sufficient to represent discourse structure in simultaneous spoken Turkish. Unfortunately, due to time and budget constraints, continuous annotation of a large-scale corpus with multiple annotators is not possible for the short term. Therefore, the immediate goal is to extract excerpts of interest that include tree-violation candidates, annotate the violations along with their immediate context adopting a PDTB-style annotation with some adjustments for Turkish and spoken language; and explore means of explaining away these violations by non-structural cohesive ties defined by Halliday and Hasan (1976). Cohesive ties include the frequently discussed anaphora (*reference* in their terms), but also include other non-structural mechanisms such as *ellipsis* and *lexical cohesion.*

3.1 Extracting tree-violation candidates

The first step of the study is to examine the structural configurations in the TDB. Although the TDB is a written text source, it contains texts from multiple genres; and in some genres such as novels, stories and interviews, dialogues are annotated for discourse structure. We expect the TDB annotations to provide some insight that can be transferred to spoken language. For example, if a certain discourse connective, a particular attribution verb or some specific type of embedded clause seem to participate frequently in tree-violations in the TDB, searching for instances of that particular elements in spoken data may considerably hasten the search for tree-violation candidates.

The second step is the continuous annotation of small pieces of spoken data. The goal of this step is not to produce a fully annotated spoken corpus, but rather to gather some insight into the structures that are unique to spoken data. By annotating randomly selected small pieces of spoken data, we aim to discover structures that are unique to spoken data that cannot be extracted form the TDB. Like the first step, the goal is to identify elements that are likely to result in tree-violations that can be searched for in large amounts of unannotated data.

The last step is obviously to look for the identified elements in the first two phases in larger amounts of spoken data and annotate them. Currently considered spoken resources are the METU Spoken Turkish Corpus (Ruhi and Karadaş 2009) and freely available podcasts.

3.2 Anticipated adjustments to the PDTB annotation scheme

The TDB has already made some adjustments for Turkish on the PDTB style. One major adjustment is to annotate phrasal expressions that include deictic expressions (such as *bu sebeple* 'for this reason') as discourse connectives. Although the PDTB annotates some phrasal and multipart connectives, deictic and productive phrasal expressions such as *that's because* or *the reason is* were annotated as alternative lexicalizations rather than lexicalized discourse predicates. In the TDB, such expressions are annotated as discourse connectives because of the structural similarity between deictic phrasal expressions and subordinating discourse connectives. In addition, a *shared* span label was introduced to accommodate for text spans that belong to both arguments, such as sentential adverbials or subjects of subordinate clauses. Finally, in an ongoing attempt to add sense annotations to the TDB, some new sense labels such as OBJECTION and CORRECTION were added to the PDTB sense hierarchy.

In addition to Turkish-specific changes, we will consider adopting speech-specific changes such as the non-adjacent implicit connectives and the *repetition* label by Tonelli (2010) as needed.

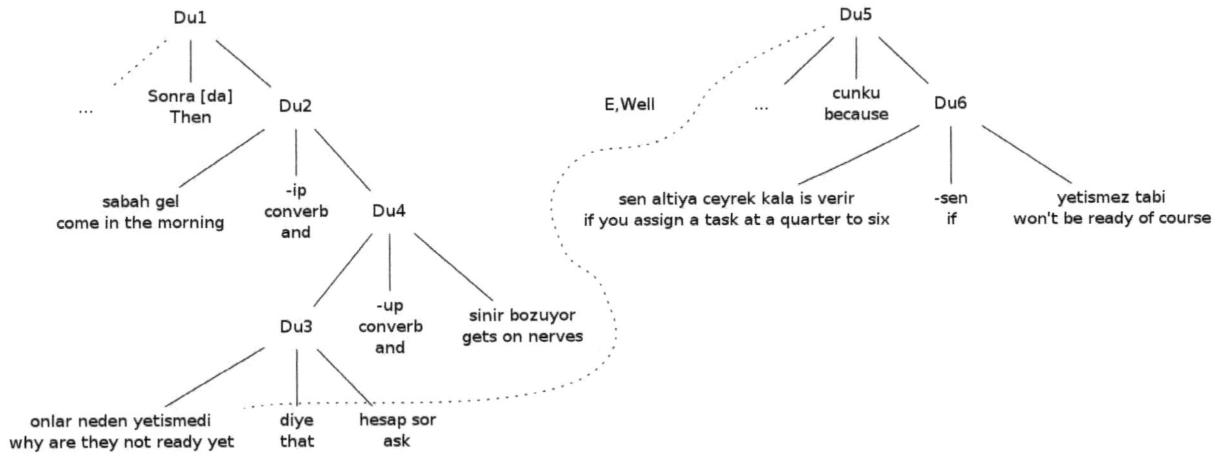

Figure2: An attempt at building a tree for (5). The first argument of *çünkü* in Du5 is either recovered from Du3 by non-structural means, or taken structurally form Du3, resulting in *pure crossing* and depending on the decision to annotate attribution as a discourse annotation or not, either *shared argument* or *properly contained argument.*

3.3 A sample tree-violation candidate

A sample excerpt of interest is (5). The context is that the speaker is complaining that the project manager assigns new tasks right before the end of working hours.

(5) Sonra da sabah gelip *onlar neden yetişmedi* diye hesap sorup sinir bozuyor. E, çünkü **sen altıya çeyrek kala iş verirsen yetişmez tabi**.

Then he comes in the morning and asks *why they are not ready yet* and (thus) he gets on my nerves. Well, because **if you assign the task at a quarter to six o'clock, they won't be ready of course**.

In (5), the first argument of the connective *çünkü* 'because' is the complement of asking, and is embedded in a sequence of events. Most importantly, it is neither the first nor the last event in the sequence, so structurally it should not be available to *çünkü*.

Once a tree-violation candidate such as (5) is identified, it will be analyzed to see if a plausible tree structure can be constructed, or the violation can be explained away by non-structural mechanisms or speech-specific features such as intonation. In this case, there doesn't seem to be an anaphoric explanation to get rid of the crossing dependency. However, left hand side argument of *çünkü* is embedded in a verb of attribution.

"Why are they not ready yet?" and the answer "Because if you give the task at a quarter to six o'clock, they won't be ready of course." make up a sub-discourse distinct from the structure of the main discourse. Another non-structural explanation is *ellipsis*, where the missing argument of *çünkü* is recovered from the preceding context. *Repetition* (an element of lexical cohesion) of *yetişmek* 'to catch up, be ready', may play a role in the recovery of the missing argument. At this point, we confine ourselves to identifying possible explanations, but refrain from committing ourselves to any one of the explanations. Further research should reveal whether this is a frequent dependency type a. for *çünkü* 'because', b. for lexically reinforced *ellipsis* and c. for arguments of attribution verbs d. for Turkish discourse, or e. for spontaneous speech. Each of this possibilities will have different ramifications, ranging from a discourse adverbial interpretation of *çünkü* 'because' to a graph structure for spoken discourse.

4 Conclusion

Whether tree structure is sufficient to represent discourse relations is an open question that will benefit from diverse studies in multiple languages and modalities. Here we have presented some of the arguments for and against tree structure in discourse. The current study aims to reveal the constraints in simultaneous spoken Turkish discourse structure. The proposed framework for discourse structure analysis is based on PDTB-style, with adjustments for Turkish and spoken language. The adjustments will be based on the existing PDTB-style studies in

Turkish and simultaneous speech, although they are likely to evolve further as research progresses. The methodology for the study is to search for possible tree-violations, and try to apply the explanations in the literature to explain them away. The violations that cannot be plausibly explained away by non-structural mechanisms should be accommodated by the final discourse model.

Acknowledgements

We gratefully acknowledge the support of Turkish Scientific and Technological Research Council of Turkey (TUBITAK) and METU Scientific Research Fund (no. BAP-07-04-2011-005) for the Turkish Discourse Bank.

References

Berfin Aktaş, Cem Bozşahin, Deniz Zeyrek. 2010. Discourse Relation Configurations in Turkish and an Annotation Environment. *Proc. LAW IV - The Fourth Linguistic Annotation Workshop*.

Nicholas Asher. 1993. *Reference to Abstract Objects in Discourse*. Kluwer Academic Publishers.

Jason Baldridge, Alex Lascarides. 2005. Annotating Discourse Structure for Robust Semantic Interpretation. *Proc. 6th International Workshop on Computational Semantics.*

Markus Egg, Gisela Redeker. 2008. Underspecified Discourse Representation. In A. Benz and P. Kuhnlein (eds) *Constraints in Discourse* (117-138). Benjamins: Amsterdam.

Markus Egg, Gisela Redeker. 2010. How Complex is Discourse Structure? *Proc. 7th International Conference on Language Resources and Evaluation (LREC 2010)* pp. 1619–23.

Katherine Forbes, Eleni Miltsakaki, Rashmi Prasad, Anoop Sarkar, Aravind K. Joshi. 2003. D-LTAG System: Discourse Parsing with a Lexicalized Tree-Adjoining Grammar. *Journal of Logic, Language and Information*, 12(3), 261–279.

Katherine Forbes-Riley, Bonnie Webber, Aravind K. Joshi. 2005. Computing Discourse Semantics: The Predicate-Argument Semantics of Discourse Connectives in D-LTAG. *Journal of Semantics*, 23, 55-106.

Michael A. K. Halliday, Ruqaiya Hasan. 1976. *Cohesion in English*. London: Longman.

Jerry R. Hobbs. 1985. On the Coherence and Structure of Discourse. *Report CSLI-85-37, Center for Study of Language and Information.*

Aravind K. Joshi. 1987. An Introduction to Tree Adjoining Grammar. In A. Manaster- Ramer (Ed.), *Mathematics of Language*. Amsterdam: John Benjamins.

Alistair Knott, Jon Oberlander, Michael O'Donnel, Chris Mellish. 2001. Beyond elaboration: The interaction of relations and focus in coherent text. In T. Sanders, J. Schilperoord & W. Spooren (Eds.), *Text Representation:Linguistic and psycholinguistic aspects* (181-196): John Benjamins Publishing.

Alan Lee, Rashmi Prasad, Aravind K. Joshi, Nikhil Dinesh, Bonnie Webber. 2006. Complexity of dependencies in discourse: are dependencies in discourse more complex than in syntax? *Proc. 5th Workshop on Treebanks and Linguistic Theory (TLT'06).*

Alan Lee, Rashmi Prasad, Aravind K. Joshi, Bonnie Webber. 2008. Departures from tree structures in discourse. *Proc. Workshop on Constraints in Discourse III.*

William C. Mann, Sandra A. Thompson. 1988. Rhetorical structure theory: Toward a functional theory of text organization. *Text,* 8(3), 243-281.

Rashmi Prasad, Nikhil Dinesh, Alan Lee, Eleni Miltsakaki, Livio Robaldo, Aravind K. Joshi, Bonnie Webber. 2008. The Penn Discourse Treebank 2.0. *Proc. LREC'08 - The sixth international conference on Language Resources and Evaluation.*

Şükriye Ruhi, Derya Çokal Karadaş. 2009. Features for an internet accessible corpus of spoken Turkish discourse. *Working Papers in Corpus-based Linguistics and Language Education* 3, 311-320.

Amanda Stent. 2000. Rhetorical structure in dialog. *Proc. 2nd International Natural Language Generation Conference (INLG'2000). Student paper.*

Sara Tonelli, Giuseppe Riccardi, Rashmi Prasad, Aravind Joshi. 2010. Annotation of Discourse Relations for Conversational Spoken Dialogues. In *Proceedings of the Seventh International Conference on Language Resources and Evaluation (LREC).*

Bonnie Webber, Matthew Stone, Aravind K. Joshi, Alistair Knott. 2003. Anaphora and discourse structure. *Computational Linguistics*. 29 (4):545-587.

Bonnie Webber. 2004. D-LTAG: Extending Lexicalized TAG to Discourse. Cognitive Science, 28(5), 751-779.

Bonnie Webber, Markus Egg, Valia Kordoni. 2011. Discourse structure and language technology. *Natural Language Engineering,* doi: 10.1017/S1351324911000337, Published online by Cambridge University Press 08 December 2011.

Florian Wolf, Edward Gibson. 2005. Representing discourse coherence: a corpus-based study. *Computational Linguistics* 31: 249–87.

Deniz Zeyrek, Işın Demirşahin, Ayışığı Sevdik-Çallı, Hale Ögel Balaban, İhsan Yalçınkaya, Ümit Deniz Turan. 2010. The annotation scheme of Turkish discourse bank and an evaluation of inconsistent annotations. *Proc. 4th Linguistic Annotation Workshop (LAW IV).*

A Generic Framework for Multiword Expressions Treatment: from Acquisition to Applications

Carlos Ramisch
Federal University of Rio Grande do Sul (Brazil)
GETALP — LIG, University of Grenoble (France)
`ceramisch@inf.ufrgs.br`

Abstract

This paper presents an open and flexible methodological framework for the automatic acquisition of multiword expressions (MWEs) from monolingual textual corpora. This research is motivated by the importance of MWEs for NLP applications. After briefly presenting the modules of the framework, the paper reports extrinsic evaluation results considering two applications: computer-aided lexicography and statistical machine translation. Both applications can benefit from automatic MWE acquisition and the expressions acquired automatically from corpora can both speed up and improve their quality. The promising results of previous and ongoing experiments encourage further investigation about the optimal way to integrate MWE treatment into these and many other applications.

SRC	*I* **paid** *my poor parents* **a visit**
MT	*J'ai* **payé** *mes pauvres parents* **une visite**
REF	*J'ai* **rendu visite** *à mes pauvres parents*
SRC	*Students pay* **an arm and a leg** *to park on campus*
MT	*Les étudiants paient* **un bras et une jambe** *pour se garer sur le campus*
REF	*Les étudiants paient* **les yeux de la tête** *pour se garer sur le campus*
SRC	*It shares the* **translation-invariance and homogeneity properties** *with the central moment*
MT	*Il partage la* **traduction-invariance et propriétés d'homogénéité** *avec le moment central*
REF	*Il partage les* **propriétés d'invariance par translation et d'homogénéité** *avec le moment central*

Table 1: Examples of SMT errors due to MWEs.

1 Introduction

Multiword expressions (MWEs) range over linguistic constructions such as idioms (*to pay an arm and a leg*), fixed phrases (*rock 'n' roll*) and noun compounds (*dry ice*). There is no unique and widely accepted definition for the term *multiword expression*. It can be an "arbitrary and recurrent word combination" (Smadja, 1993) or "a syntactic and semantic unit whose exact and unambiguous meaning or connotation cannot be derived directly from the meaning or connotation of its components" (Choueka, 1988) or simply an "idiosyncratic interpretation that crosses word boundaries (or spaces)" (Sag et al., 2002). MWEs lie in the fuzzy zone between lexicon and syntax, thus constituting a real challenge for NLP systems. In addition, they are very pervasive, occurring frequently in everyday language as well as in specialised communications. Some common properties of MWEs are:[1]

- **Arbitrariness**: sometimes valid constructions are not acceptable because people do not use them. Smadja (1993, p. 143–144) illustrates this by presenting 8 different ways of referring to the Dow Jones index, among which only 4 are used.
- **Institutionalisation**: MWEs are recurrent, as they correspond to conventional ways of saying things. Jackendoff (1997) estimates that they compose half of the entries of a speaker's lexicon, and Sag et al. (2002) point out that this may be an underestimate if we consider domain-specific MWEs.
- **Limited semantic variability**: MWEs do not undergo the same semantic compositionality rules as ordinary word combinations. This is expressed in terms of **(i) non-compositionality**, as the meaning of the whole expression often cannot be directly inferred from the meaning of the parts composing it, **(ii) non-substitutability**, as it is not possible to replace part of an MWE by a related (synonym/equivalent) word or construction, and **(iii) no word-for-word translation**.

[1]These are not binary yes/no flags, but values in a continuum going from flexible word combinations to prototypical fixed expressions.

- **Limited syntactic variability**: standard grammatical rules do not apply to MWEs. This can be expressed in terms of **(i) lexicalisation**, as one cannot list all MWEs in the lexicon (undergeneration) nor include them all in the grammar (overgeneration) and **(ii) extragrammaticality**, as MWEs are unpredictable and seem "weird" for a second language learner who only knows general rules.[2]
- **Heterogeneity**: MWEs are hard to define because they encompass a large amount of phenomena. Thus, NLP applications cannot use a unified approach and need to rely on some typology[3].

In this paper, I adopt the definition by Calzolari et al. (2002), who define MWEs as:

> different but related phenomena [which] can be described as a sequence[4] of words that acts as a single unit at some level of linguistic analysis.

This generic and intentionally vague definition can be narrowed down according to the application needs. For example, for the statistical machine translation (MT) system[5] used in the examples shown in Table 1, an MWE is any sequence of words which, when not translated as a unit, generates errors: ungrammatical or unnatural verbal constructions (sentence 1), awkward literal translations of idioms (sentence 2) and problems of lexical choice and word order in specialised texts (sentence 3). These examples illustrate the importance of correctly dealing with MWEs in MT applications and, more generally, MWEs can speed up and help remove ambiguities in many current NLP applications, for example:

- **Lexicography**: Church and Hanks (1990) used a lexicographic environment as their evaluation scenario, comparing manual and intuitive research with the automatic association ratio they proposed.
- **Word sense disambiguation**: MWEs tend to be less polysemous than simple words. Finlayson and Kulkarni (2011) exemplify that the word *world* has 9 senses in Wordnet 1.6, *record* has 14, but *world record* has only 1.
- **POS tagging and parsing**: recent work in parsing and POS tagging indicates that MWEs can help remove syntactic ambiguities (Seretan, 2008).
- **Information retrieval**: when MWEs like *pop star* are indexed as a unit, the accuracy of the system improves on multiword queries (Acosta et al., 2011).

[2]Examples of MWEs that breach standard grammatical rules include *kingdom come* and *by and large*.

[3]For example, Smadja (1993) classifies them according to syntactic function while Sag et al. (2002) classify them according to flexibility.

[4]Although they define MWEs as "sequences", assuming contiguity, we assume "sets" of words for greater generality.

[5]Automatic translations (MT) by Google (`http://translate.google.com/`) on 2012/02/18. Reference (REF) by native speaker.

2 Thesis contributions

Despite the importance of MWEs in several applications, they are often neglected in the design and construction of real-life systems. In 1993, Smadja pointed out that "... although disambiguation was originally considered as a performance task, the collocations retrieved have not been used for any specific computational task." Most of the recent and current research in the MWE community still focuses on MWE acquisition instead of integration of automatically acquired or manually compiled resources into applications. The main contribution of my thesis is that it represents a step toward the integration of automatically extracted MWEs into real-life applications. Concretely, my contributions can be classified in two categories: first, I propose a unified, open and flexible *methodological framework* (§ 3) for automatic MWE acquisition from corpora; and second, I am performing an intrinsic and extrinsic *evaluation of MWE acquisition* (§ 4), dissecting the influence of the different types of resources employed in the acquisition on the quality of the MWEs. The results of ongoing experiments are interesting but further work is needed to better understand the contributions of MWEs to the systems (§ 5).

Methodological Framework To date, there is no agreement on whether there is a single best method for MWE acquisition, or whether a different subset of methods works better for a given MWE type. Most of recent work on MWE treatment focuses on candidate extraction from preprocessed text (Seretan, 2008) and on the automatic filtering and ranking through association measures (Evert, 2004; Pecina, 2010), but few authors provide a whole picture of the MWE treatment pipeline. One of the advantages of the framework I propose is that it models the whole acquisition process with modular tasks that can be chained in several ways, each task having multiple available techniques. Therefore, it is highly customisable and allows for a large number of parameters to be tuned according to the target MWE types. Moreover, the techniques I have developed do not depend on a fixed length of candidate expression nor on adjacency assumptions, as the words in an expression might occur several words away. Thanks to this flexibility, this methodology can be easily applied to virtually any language, MWE type and domain, not strictly depending on a given formalism or tool[6]. Intuitively, for a given language, if some preprocessing tools like POS taggers and/or parsers are available, the results will be much better than running the methods on raw text. But since such tools are not available for all languages, the methodology was conceived to be applicable even in the absence of preprocessing.

[6]However, it is designed to deal with languages that use spaces to separate words. Thus, when working with Chinese, Japanese, or even with German compounds, some additional preprocessing is required.

Evaluation of MWE Acquisition Published results comparing MWE extraction techniques usually evaluate them on small controlled data sets using objective measures such as precision, recall and mean average precision (Schone and Jurafsky, 2001; Pearce, 2002; Evert and Krenn, 2005). On the one hand, the results of *intrinsic evaluation* are often vague or inconclusive: although they shed some light on the optimal parameters for the given scenario, they are hard to generalise and cannot be directly applied to other configurations. The quality of acquired MWEs as measured by objective criteria depends on the language, domain and type of the target construction, on corpus size and genre, on already available resources[7], on the applied filters, preprocessing steps, etc. On the other hand, *extrinsic evaluation* consists of inserting acquired MWEs into a real NLP application and evaluating the impact of this new data on the overall performance of the system. For instance, it may be easier to ask a human annotator to evaluate the output of an MT system than to ask whether a sequence of words constitutes an MWE. Thus, another original contribution of my thesis is application-oriented extrinsic evaluation of MWE acquisition on two study cases: computer-aided lexicography and statistical machine translation. My goal is to investigate (1) how much the MWEs impact on the application and (2) what is (are) the best way(s) of integrating them in the complex pipeline of the target application.

3 MWE Extraction

Among early work on developing methods for MWE identification, there is that of Smadja (1993). He proposed and developed a tool called Xtract, aimed at general-purpose collocation extraction from text using a combination of *n*-grams and a mutual information measure. On general-purpose texts, Xtract has a precision of around 80%. Since then, many advances have been made, either looking at MWEs in general (Dias, 2003), or focusing on specific MWE types, such as collocations, phrasal verbs and compound nouns. A popular type-independent approach to MWE identification is to use statistical association measures, which have been applied to the task with varying degrees of success (Evert and Krenn, 2005). One of the advantages of this approach is that it is language independent. This is particularly important since although work on MWEs in several languages has been reported, e.g. Dias (2003) for Portuguese and Evert and Krenn (2005) for German, work on English still seems to predominate.

I propose a new framework called `mwetoolkit`, described in Figure 1, which integrates multiple techniques and covers the whole pipeline of MWE acquisition. One can preprocess a raw monolingual corpus, if tools are available for the target language, enriching it with POS tags, lemmas and dependency syntax. Then, based on expert linguistic knowledge, intuition, empiric observation and/or examples, one defines multilevel patterns in a formalism similar to regular expressions to describe the target MWEs. The application of these patterns on an indexed corpus generates a list of candidate MWEs. For filtering, a plethora of methods is available, ranging from simple frequency thresholds to stopword lists and sophisticated association measures. Finally, the resulting filtered candidates are either directly injected into an NLP application or further manually validated before application. An alternative use for the validated candidates is to train a machine learning model which can be applied on new corpora in order to automatically identify and extract MWEs based on the characteristics of the previously acquired ones. For further details, please refer to the website of the framework[8] and to previous publications (Ramisch et al., 2010a; Ramisch et al., 2010b).

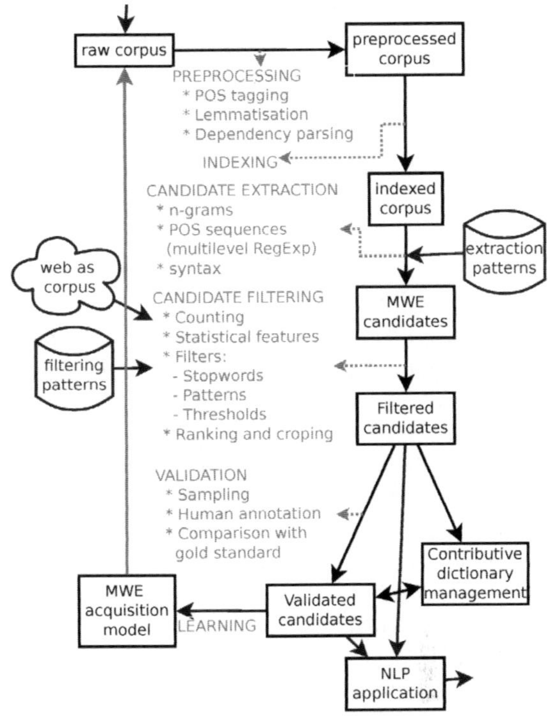

Figure 1: Framework for MWE acquisition from corpora

4 Application-oriented evaluation

In this section, I present summarised results of extrinsic quantitative and qualitative evaluation of the framework for MWE acquisition propose in § 3. The target applications are computer-aided lexicography (§ 4.1) and statistical machine translation (§ 4.2).

[7]It is useless to acquire MWEs already present in the dictionary.

[8]`http://mwetoolkit.sf.net`

Language	Type	Corpus (words)	Candidates	Final MWEs	Publication
English	PV	Europarl (13M)	5.3K	875	(Ramisch et al., 2012)
French	NC	Europarl (14.5M)	104K	3,746	(Ramisch et al., 2012)
Greek	NC	Europarl (26M)	25K	815	(Linardaki et al., 2010)
Portuguese	CP	PLN-BR-FULL (29M)	407K	773	(Duran et al., 2011)

Table 2: MWE acquisition applied to lexicography

4.1 Computer-aided Lexicography

In this evaluation, I collaborated with colleagues who are experienced linguists and lexicographers, in order to create new lexical resources containing MWEs. The languages of the resources are English, French, Greek and Portuguese. Table 2 summarises the outcomes of each evaluation. The created data sets are freely available.[9, 10]

We extracted English phrasal verbs (PVs) from the English portion of the Europarl corpus[11]. We considered a PV as being formed by a verb (except *to be* and *to have*) followed by a prepositional particle[12] not further than 5 words after it[13] This resulted in 5,302 phrasal verb candidates occurring more than once in the corpus, from which 875 were automatically identified as true PVs and the others are currently under manual validation. Analogously, the French noun compounds (NCs) were extracted from Europarl using the following pattern: a noun followed by either an adjective or a prepositional complement[14]. After filtering out candidates that occur once in the corpus, we obtained 3,746 MWE candidates and part of the remaining candidates will be manually analysed in the future.

For Greek, in particular, considerable work has been done to study the linguistic properties of MWEs, but computational approaches are still limited (Fotopoulou et al., 2008). In our experiments, we extracted from the POS-tagged Greek part of the Europarl corpus words matching the following patterns: adjective-noun, noun-noun, noun-determiner-noun, noun-preposition-noun, preposition-noun-noun, noun-adjective-noun and noun-conjunction-noun. The candidates were counted in two corpora and annotated with four association measures, and the top 150 according to each measure where annotated by three native speakers, that is, each annotator judged around 1,200 candidates and in the end the annotations were joined, creating a lexicon with 815 Greek nominal MWEs.

Finally, the goal of the work with Portuguese complex predicates (CPs) was to perform a qualitative analysis of these constructions. Therefore, we POS-tagged the PLN-BR-FULL corpus[15] and extracted sequences of words matching the patterns: verb-[determiner]-noun-preposition, verb-preposition-noun, verb-[preposition/determiner]-adverb and verb-adjective. The extraction process resulted in a list of 407,014 candidates which were further filtered using statistical association measures. Thus, an expert human annotator manually validated 12,545 candidates from which 699 were annotated as compositional verbal expressions and 74 as idiomatic verbal expressions. Afterwards, a fine-grained analysis of each extraction pattern was conducted with the goal of finding correlations between syntactic flexibility and semantic properties such as compositionality.

4.2 Statistical Machine Translation (SMT)

Incorporating even simple treatments for MWEs in SMT systems can improve translation quality. For instance, Carpuat and Diab (2010) adopt two complementary strategies for integrating MWEs: a static strategy of single-tokenisation that treats MWEs as word-with-spaces and a dynamic strategy that adds a count for the number of MWEs in the source phrase. They found that both strategies result in improvement of translation quality, which suggests that SMT phrases alone do not model all MWE information. Morin and Daille (2010) obtained an improvement of 33% in the French–Japanese translation of MWEs with a morphologically-based compositional method for backing-off when there is not enough data in a dictionary to translate a MWE (e.g. *chronic fatigue syndrome* decomposed as *[chronic fatigue] [syndrome]*, *[chronic] [fatigue syndrome]* or *[chronic] [fatigue] [syndrome]*). For translating from and to morphologically rich languages like German, where a compound is in fact a single token formed through concatenation, Stymne (2011) splits the compound into its single word components prior to translation and then applies some post-processing, like the reordering or merging of the components, after translation. She obtains improvements in BLEU from 21.63 to 22.12 in English–Swedish and from 19.31 to 19.73 in English–German.

[9] `http://multiword.sourceforge.net/PHITE.php?sitesig=FILES&page=FILES_20_Data_Sets`

[10] `http://www.inf.ufrgs.br/~ceramisch/?page=downloads/mwecompare`

[11] `http://statmt.org/europarl`

[12] *up, off, down, back, away, in, on.*

[13] Even though the particle might occur further than 5 positions away, such cases are sufficiently rare to be ignored in this experiment.

[14] Prepositions *de*, *à* and *en* followed by optionally determined noun.

[15] `www.nilc.icmc.usp.br/plnbr`

	% Good	% Acceptable	% Incorrect
Baseline	0.53	0.36	0.11
TOK	0.55	0.29	0.16
PV?	0.50	0.39	0.11
PART	0.53	0.36	0.11
VERB	0.53	0.36	0.11
BILEX	0.50	0.29	0.20

Table 3: Evaluation of translation of phrasal verbs in test set.

In the current experiments, a standard non factored phrase-based SMT system was built using the open-source Moses toolkit with parameters similar to those of the baseline system for the 2011 WMT campaign. [16]. For training, we used the English–Portuguese Europarl v6 (EP) corpus, with 1.7M sentences and around 50M words. The training data contains the first 200K sentences tokenized and lowercased, resulting in 152,235 parallel sentences and around 3.1M words. The whole Portuguese corpus was used as training data for 5-gram language model built with SRILM. Phrasal verbs were automatically identified using the jMWE tool and a dictionary of PVs. We compared the following five strategies for the integration of automatically identified phrasal verbs in the system:

- TOK: before translation, rearrange the verb and the particle in a joint configuration and transform them into a single token with underscore (e.g. *call him up* into *call_up him*).
- PV?: add a binary feature to each bi-phrase indicating whether a source phrasal verb has been detected in it or not.
- PART: replace the particle by the one most frequently used with the target verb, using a web-based language model with a symmetric windows of 1 to 5 words around the particle.
- VERB: modify the form of the Portuguese verb (gerund or infinitive), according to the form detected on the English side.
- BILEX (or *bilingual lexicon*): augment the phrase table of the baseline system with 179,133 new bilingual phrases from an English–Portuguese phrasal verb lexicon.

Table 3 shows the preliminary results of a human evaluation performed on a test set of 100 sentences. The sentences were inspected and we verified that, while some translations improve with the integration strategies, others are degraded. No absolute improvement was observed, but we believe that this is due to the fact that our evaluation needs to consider more fine-grained classes of phrasal verbs instead of mixing them all in the same test set. Additionally, we would need to annotate more data in order to obtain more representative results. These hypotheses motivate us to continue our investigation in order to obtain a deeper understanding the impact of each integration strategy on each step of the SMT system.

[16] www.statmt.org/wmt11/baseline.html

5 Future Experiments and Perspectives

In this paper, I described an open framework for the automatic acquisition of MWEs from corpora. What distinguishes it from related work is that it provides an integrated environment covering the whole acquisition pipeline. For each module, there are multiple available techniques which are flexible, portable and can be combined in several ways. The usefulness of the framework is then presented in terms of extrinsic application-based evaluation. I presented summarised results of ongoing experiments in computer-aided lexicography and in SMT.

Although our results are promising, the experiments on SMT need further investigation. I am currently applying syntax-based identification and analysing word alignment and translation table entries for a set of prototypical MWEs, in order to obtain a better understanding of the impact of each integration strategy on the system. Moreover, I would like to pursue previous experiments on bilingual MWE acquisition from parallel and comparable resources. Finally, I would like to experiment on MWE simplification (e.g. replacing a multiword verb like *go back* by its simplex form *regress*) as preprocessing for SMT, in order to improve translation quality by making the source language look more like the target language.As these improvements depend in the MT paradigm, I would also like to evaluate strategies for the integration of verbal MWEs in expert MT systems.

In spite of a large amount of work in the area, the treatment of MWEs in NLP applications is still an open and challenging problem. This is not surprising, given their complex and heterogeneous behaviour (Sag et al., 2002). At the beginning of the 2000's, Schone and Jurafsky (2001) asked whether the identification of MWEs was a solved problem, and the answer that paper gave was 'no, it is not'. The MWE workshop series have shown that this is still the case, listing several challenges in MWE treatment like lexical representation and application-oriented evaluation. Therefore, I believe that my thesis will be a significant step toward the full integration of MWE treatment in NLP applications, but there is still a long road to go.

Acknowledgements

This work was partly funded by the CAMELEON project (CAPES–COFECUB 707-11) and by a Ph.D. grant from the French Ministry for Higher Education and Research. I would like to thank my supervisors Aline Villavicencio and Christian Boitet, as well as the colleagues who contributed to this work: Evita Linardaki, Valia Kordoni, Magali Sanchez Duran and Vitor De Araujo.

References

Otavio Acosta, Aline Villavicencio, and Viviane Moreira. 2011. Identification and treatment of multiword expressions applied to information retrieval. In Valia Kordoni, Carlos Ramisch, and Aline Villavicencio, editors, *Proc.of the ALC Workshop on MWEs: from Parsing and Generation to the Real World (MWE 2011)*, pages 101–109, Portland, OR, USA, Jun. ACL.

Nicoleta Calzolari, Charles Fillmore, Ralph Grishman, Nancy Ide, Alessandro Lenci, Catherine Macleod, and Antonio Zampolli. 2002. Towards best practice for multiword expressions in computational lexicons. In *Proc. of the Third LREC (LREC 2002)*, pages 1934–1940, Las Palmas, Canary Islands, Spain, May. ELRA.

Marine Carpuat and Mona Diab. 2010. Task-based evaluation of multiword expressions: a pilot study in statistical machine translation. In *Proc. of HLT: The 2010 Annual Conf. of the NAACL (NAACL 2003)*, pages 242–245, Los Angeles, California, Jun. ACL.

Yaacov Choueka. 1988. Looking for needles in a haystack or locating interesting collocational expressions in large textual databases. In *RIAO'88*, pages 609–624.

Kenneth Ward Church and Patrick Hanks. 1990. Word association norms mutual information, and lexicography. *Comp. Ling.*, 16(1):22–29.

Gaël Dias. 2003. Multiword unit hybrid extraction. In Francis Bond, Anna Korhonen, Diana McCarthy, and Aline Villavicencio, editors, *Proc. of the ACL Workshop on MWEs: Analysis, Acquisition and Treatment (MWE 2003)*, pages 41–48, Sapporo, Japan, Jul. ACL.

Magali Sanches Duran, Carlos Ramisch, Sandra Maria Aluísio, and Aline Villavicencio. 2011. Identifying and analyzing brazilian portuguese complex predicates. In Valia Kordoni, Carlos Ramisch, and Aline Villavicencio, editors, *Proc.of the ALC Workshop on MWEs: from Parsing and Generation to the Real World (MWE 2011)*, pages 74–82, Portland, OR, USA, Jun. ACL.

Stefan Evert and Brigitte Krenn. 2005. Using small random samples for the manual evaluation of statistical association measures. *Comp. Speech & Lang. Special issue on MWEs*, 19(4):450–466.

Stefan Evert. 2004. *The Statistics of Word Cooccurrences: Word Pairs and Collocations*. Ph.D. thesis, Institut für maschinelle Sprachverarbeitung, University of Stuttgart, Stuttgart, Germany.

Mark Finlayson and Nidhi Kulkarni. 2011. Detecting multiword expressions improves word sense disambiguation. In Valia Kordoni, Carlos Ramisch, and Aline Villavicencio, editors, *Proc.of the ALC Workshop on MWEs: from Parsing and Generation to the Real World (MWE 2011)*, pages 20–24, Portland, OR, USA, Jun. ACL.

Aggeliki Fotopoulou, Giorgos Giannopoulos, Maria Zourari, and Marianna Mini. 2008. Automatic recognition and extraction of multiword nominal expressions from corpora (in greek). In *Proceedings of the 29th Annual Meeting, Department of Linguistics*, Aristotle University of Thessaloniki, Greece.

Ray Jackendoff. 1997. Twistin' the night away. *Language*, 73:534–559.

Evita Linardaki, Carlos Ramisch, Aline Villavicencio, and Aggeliki Fotopoulou. 2010. Towards the construction of language resources for greek multiword expressions: Extraction and evaluation. In Stelios Piperidis, Milena Slavcheva, and Cristina Vertan, editors, *Proc. of the LREC Workshop on Exploitation of multilingual resources and tools for Central and (South) Eastern European Languages*, pages 31–40, Valetta, Malta. May.

Emmanuel Morin and Béatrice Daille. 2010. Compositionality and lexical alignment of multi-word terms. *Lang. Res. & Eval. Special Issue on Multiword expression: hard going or plain sailing*, 44(1-2):79–95, Apr.

Darren Pearce. 2002. A comparative evaluation of collocation extraction techniques. In *Proc. of the Third LREC (LREC 2002)*, Las Palmas, Canary Islands, Spain, May. ELRA.

Pavel Pecina. 2010. Lexical association measures and collocation extraction. *Lang. Res. & Eval. Special Issue on Multiword expression: hard going or plain sailing*, 44(1-2):137–158, Apr.

Carlos Ramisch, Aline Villavicencio, and Christian Boitet. 2010a. Multiword expressions in the wild? the mwetoolkit comes in handy. In Yang Liu and Ting Liu, editors, *Proc. of the 23rd COLING (COLING 2010) — Demonstrations*, pages 57–60, Beijing, China, Aug. The Coling 2010 Organizing Committee.

Carlos Ramisch, Aline Villavicencio, and Christian Boitet. 2010b. mwetoolkit: a framework for multiword expression identification. In *Proc. of the Seventh LREC (LREC 2010)*, Malta, May. ELRA.

Carlos Ramisch, Vitor De Araujo, and Aline Villavicencio. 2012. A broad evaluation of techniques for automatic acquisition of multiword expressions. In *Proc. of the ACL 2012 SRW*, Jeju, Republic of Korea, Jul. ACL.

Ivan Sag, Timothy Baldwin, Francis Bond, Ann Copestake, and Dan Flickinger. 2002. Multiword expressions: A pain in the neck for NLP. In *Proc. of the 3rd CICLing (CICLing-2002)*, volume 2276/2010 of *LNCS*, pages 1–15, Mexico City, Mexico, Feb. Springer.

Patrick Schone and Daniel Jurafsky. 2001. Is knowledge-free induction of multiword unit dictionary headwords a solved problem? In Lillian Lee and Donna Harman, editors, *Proc. of the 2001 EMNLP (EMNLP 2001)*, pages 100–108, Pittsburgh, PA USA, Jun. ACL.

Violeta Seretan. 2008. *Collocation extraction based on syntactic parsing*. Ph.D. thesis, University of Geneva, Geneva, Switzerland.

Frank A. Smadja. 1993. Retrieving collocations from text: Xtract. *Comp. Ling.*, 19(1):143–177.

Sara Stymne. 2011. Pre- and postprocessing for statistical machine translation into germanic languages. In *Proc. of the ACL 2011 SRW*, pages 12–17, Portland, OR, USA, Jun. ACL.

Towards Automatic Construction of Knowledge Bases from Chinese Online Resources

Liwei Chen, Yansong Feng, Yidong Chen, Lei Zou, Dongyan Zhao
Institute of Computer Science and Technology
Peking University
Beijing, China
{clwclw88,fengyansong,chenyidong,zoulei,zhaodongyan}@pku.edu.cn

Abstract

Automatically constructing knowledge bases from online resources has become a crucial task in many research areas. Most existing knowledge bases are built from English resources, while few efforts have been made for other languages. Building knowledge bases for Chinese is of great importance on its own right. However, simply adapting existing tools from English to Chinese yields inferior results.In this paper, we propose to create Chinese knowledge bases from online resources with less human involvement.This project will be formulated in a self-supervised framework which requires little manual work to extract knowledge facts from online encyclopedia resources in a probabilistic view.In addition, this framework will be able to update the constructed knowledge base with knowledge facts extracted from up-to-date newswire.Currently, we have obtained encouraging results in our pilot experiments that extracting knowledge facts from infoboxes can achieve a high accuracy of around 95%, which will be then used as training data for the extraction of plain webpages.

1 Introduction

As the development of world wide web (WWW), the volume of web data is growing exponentially in recent years. Most of the data are unstructured, while a few are manually structured and only a small part of them are machine-readable. How to make these data accessible and useable for end users has become a key topic in many research areas, such as information retrieval, natural language processing, semantic web(Tim et al., 2001) and so on. Among others, constructing knowledge bases (KB) from web data has been considered as a preliminary step. However, it is not trivial to extract knowledge facts from unstructured web data, especially in open domain, and the accuracy is usually not satisfactory. On the other hand, with the development of Web2.0, there are increasing volume of online encyclopedias which are collectively created by active volunteers, e.g., Wikipedia[1]. Surprisingly, experiment evidences show that the confidence of Wikipedia is even comparable with that of British Encyclopedia (Giles, 2005). Therefore, many efforts have been made to distill knowledge facts from Wikipedia or similar resources and further build KBs, for example YAGO(Suchanek et al., 2007), DBpedia(Bizer et al., 2009) and KOG(Wu and Weld, 2008).

In the literature, most KBs constructed recently are in English as it takes up an overwhelming majority on the web, while other major languages receives less attention, for example, Chinese features similar amounts of web pages with English yet is less frequently studied with regarding to building KBs. Although continuous works have been made to process English resources, building Chinese KBs is of great value on its own. To the best of our knowledge, few efforts have been made to construct a KB in Chinese until now. Despite of necessary special preprocessings, e.g., word segmentation, for Chinese, building a Chinese KB from web data is quite different from building English ones, since we have limited resources available in Chinese that are of lower

[1] http://www.wikipedia.com

quality compared to their English counterparts. This brings more difficulties than that of English. As a result, the approaches used in English may not work well in Chinese.

In this paper, we propose a new framework to build a KB in Chinese from online resources without much human involvement. Since the Chinese portion of Wikipedia is much smaller than its English part, we harvest knowledge facts from a Chinese online encyclopedia, HudongBaike[2]. HudongBaike is the largest Chinese online encyclopedia and features similar managing rules and writing styles with Wikipedia. We first obtain knowledge facts by parsing the infoboxes of HudongBaike. Then we use these triples as seeds, and adopt the idea of distant supervision(Mintz et al., 2009; Riedel et al., 2010; Yao et al., 2010) to extract more facts from other HudongBaike articles and build a KB accordingly. Moreover, to make the knowledge base more up-to-date, we also propose to propagate the KB with news events.

The rest of this paper is organized as follows: we first introduce the related work, and briefly introduce two online encyclopedias. In Section 4 we describe our framework in detail. Our current work are discussed in Section 5. In Section 6 we conclude this paper.

2 Related Work

KB construction is an important task and has attracted many research efforts from artificial intelligence, information retrieval, natural language processing, and so on. Traditional KBs are mostly manually created, including WordNet(Stark and Riesenfeld, 1998), Cyc or OpenCyc(Matuszek et al., 2006), SUMO(Niles and Pease, 2001), and also some domain-specific ontologies such as GeneOntology[3]. These KBs achieve a high accuracy since they are manually built or filtered by domain experts. However, manually creating KB is a time-consuming and labor-intensive work, and continuous annotation is required to keep the KB up-to date. Most of them thus suffers from the coverage issue in practice.

In recent years, many researchers turn to automatically extract knowledge to construct KBs. One kind of methods extract knowledge facts from general text corpus. These approaches, such as TextRunner(Banko et al., 2007) and KnowItAll(Etzioni et al., 2004), use rule based information extraction technologies to extract relations between entity pairs. Recently, TextRunner is expanded by a life long learning strategy, which can acquire new facts. Another type of approaches aims to automatically derive facts from online encyclopedias. Collectively created by many volunteers, online encyclopedias are more reliable than general web pages. They also contain semi-structured knowledge such as handcrafted infoboxes. Therefore, the accuracy of the facts extracted will be higher. Researchers utilize these semi-structured data resources for knowledge extraction, for example, YAGO extract facts from infoboxes and category names of Wikipedia, and use WordNet as its taxonomy(Suchanek et al., 2007). A similar approach is adopted by DBpedia, which also extract knowledge facts from infoboxes(Bizer et al., 2009). Unlike YAGO and DBpedia, Kylin uses the infoboxes and the Wikipedia pages containing these infoboxes to build a training set, and use machine learning methods to extract facts from plain Wikipedia articles(Wu and Weld, 2007). Although Kylin achieves a high precision, it is corpus-specific, which means it can only be used in Wikipedia-like corpora. It is noticed that all the above works focus on building an English KB, and few efforts have been made in building a Chinese one until now.

3 Online Encyclopedia

Wikipedia is known as an accurate online encyclopedia whose accuracy is comparable with Encyclopedia Britannica(Giles, 2005). It's created by thousands of volunteers around the whole world. Until now, the English version of Wikipedia has 3,878,200 content pages, making it the largest English online encyclopedia. The Chinese version contains 402,781 content pages, which is much smaller than the English version.

HudongBaike is the largest Chinese online encyclopedia with over 5 million content pages. Similarly with Wikipedia, HudongBaike is also created by volunteers, and relies on the community to ensure its quality. Many HudongBaike pages also contains

[2]http://www.hudong.com

[3]http://www.geneontology.org

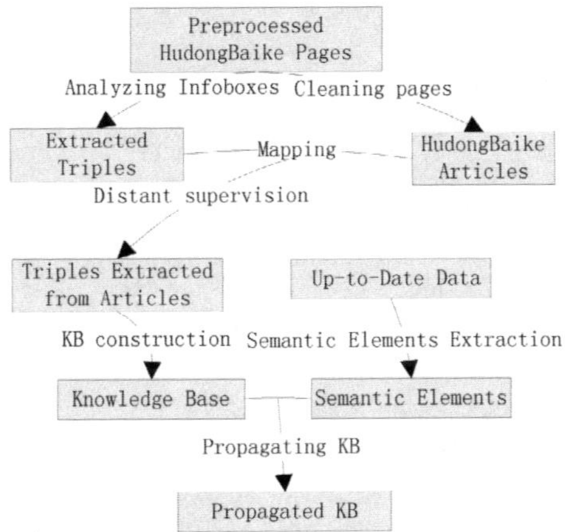

Figure 2: The framework of Our project

a hand-crafted summary box, *infobox*. An infobox summarizes the knowledge of the corresponding entity. The information in the infobox is reliable since these are collaboratively crafted by many volunteers. Figure 1 is an example page with an infobox from HudongBaike, introducing a US general 乔治・马歇尔 (George Marshall).

4 The Framework

In this paper, we formulated the KB construction task in a semi-supervised learning fashion which requires little manual annotation and supports knowledge propagation by up-to-date feeds. Because the Chinese part of Wikipedia is relatively small and may suffer from the coverage problem, we use HudongBaike to build our KB in this project. In future we may merge the Wikipedia part into our KB. After necessary preprocessings including word segmentation and named entity extraction, we are able to apply our framework shown in Figure 2.

In general, our framework contains the following steps: (1)Extracting knowledge from online encyclopedia; (2)Linking triples and building KB; (3)Propagating KB with up-to-date data.

4.1 Entity Relation Extraction

Compared to other resources on the Web, online encyclopedias contain less noises and feature more regular structures, thus are considered easier for us to extract knowledge facts.

Analyzing Infoboxes As mentioned before, many HudongBaike pages contains an infobox, which has high accuracy and can be used directly for relation extraction. We can conveniently parse these infoboxes into $< S, P, O >$ triples. For example, from the first entry of this infobox, we can derive the following triple: $<$ 乔治・马歇尔，出生地，尤尼恩敦 $>$($< GeorgeMarshall, BirthPlace, Uniontown >$). The precision of the extraction is over 95%, and these triples can form a valuable knowledge source.

Extracting relations with Distant Supervision Extracting knowledge from infoboxes is efficient and can achieve a high precision. However, many web pages in HudongBaike do not have infoboxes. There is much richer knowledge in the main articles of HudongBaike, which we should also take into consideration.

Extracting knowledge from unstructured articles is a challenging task. Traditionally, researchers use manually created templates to extract relations. These templates need lots of human efforts and are domain-specific. Recent methods trend to rely on machine learning models, which need a large amount of labeled data. One idea is to utilize the infoboxes to form the training data set, and train an extractor to extract relations from the pages without an infobox(Wu and Weld, 2007). However, the relations extracted from a page are restricted to the infobox template used by the current page category, and their subject must be the entity that this page describes. For example, when we extract relations from the page of 查克・叶格 (Charles Yeager, Ace of US in WWII) which does not contain an infobox, the subject of these relations must be Charles Yeager, and we can only extract the relation types listed in infobox template for a military person. As a result, this method can only be used in online encyclopedias in a Wikipedia style, and the recall will be relatively low.

Distant supervision is widely used in relation extraction in recent years. It hardly need any manual work, and can overcome the above problems. It can be used in any reliable corpus, and doesn't have the strict restrictions as previous methods. We adopt its idea in our framework. The basic assumption of distant supervision is the sentences containing two en-

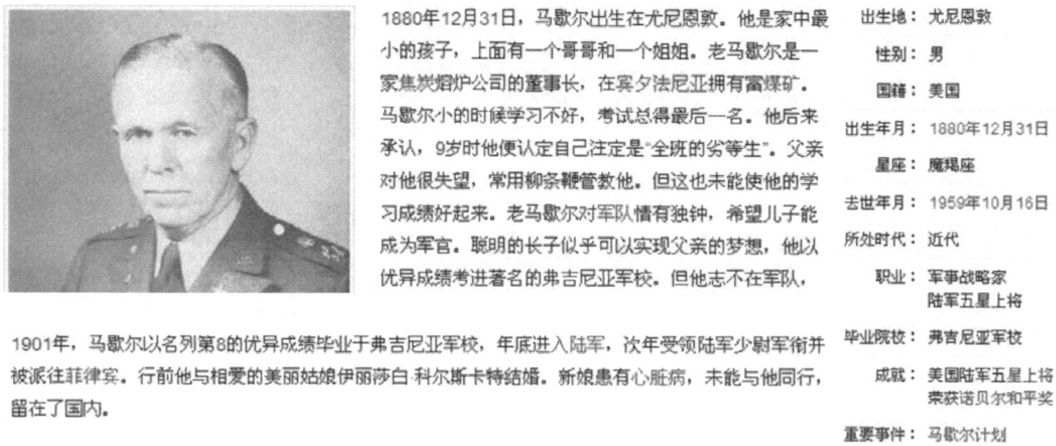

Figure 1: A HudongBaike page about a US general George Marshall

tities should express the relation between them more or less. It only needs a reliable seed KB (in the form of relation triples) and a corpus. Here, we can use the knowledge facts extracted from infoboxes previously as the seed KB, and the articles of HudongBaike as text corpus. For each triple in the seed KB, we generate positive training data by finding sentences containing both its subject and object in the corpus. For example, we can map the first entry in Figure 1 to the sentence 1880年12月31日，马歇尔出生在尤尼恩敦 (On December 31th, 1880, Marshall was born in Uniontown). The negative training data can be generated by randomly select some sentences which contain neither of the subject and the object. A predictive model such as logistic regression model is trained with the training data. We can use the model to give predictions for the relations in a textual knowledge source. For a HudongBaike page, we should decide the entity pairs we are interested in. A simple strategy is to select all entity pairs. But it will be time-consuming, and may suffer from weak-related entity pairs. So we extract topic entities which have high *tfidf* weights from this page, and generate entity pairs under the restriction that they must contain at least one topic entity. For each entity pair, we find the sentences which contain both the subject and object and use the predictive model to give the possible relations between them and the confidence of the relations.

However, the predictions of distant supervision is less accurate than those of supervised methods. So we should adopt some heuristics to filter the relations extracted. An easy strategy is to set up a threshold for relation confidences to avoid uncertain relations and improve the precision. We adopt this method in our project. Furthermore, we can also use the strategies of Riedel et al. (2010) or Yao et al. (2010).

4.2 Knowledge Base Construction

After the relation extraction, we must link the extracted knowledge triples in order to construct the knowledge base. In our scenario this linking task can be formulated as: given a base KB, a bunch of newly extracted knowledge triples with the sentences describing them and their contexts, the task of entity linking aims to link each of the entity mentions in the plain texts (these sentences mentioned above) to its corresponding entity in the base KB. At the very beginning, we initiate a base KB by using the taxonomy of HudongBaike thus are able to map relations between entities into the KB through entity linking.

In online encyclopedias, the synonyms of an entity are represented by redirect links. Synonyms are important in entity linking because they provide alternative names for entities, and we may miss some mappings without them. For example, we have an entity 美利坚合众国 (United States of America) in the KB, and an mention 美国 (USA) in a piece of text. Redirect links can tell us that we can create a mapping between them. Basically, for each mention, we can find matching candidates for them in a KB through exact matching. However, if we cannot find an exact match for a mention, we will try fuzzy matching since a mention may not match exactly with its referent entity in KB.

Now we need to solve the entity linking task. Traditional methods did not exploit global interdependence between entity linking decisions. We thus adopt the collective entity linking approach of Han et al. (2011) to solve this problem. This method captures the rich semantic relatedness knowledge between entities, and take the interdependence of linking decisions into consideration. They construct a graph by linking name mentions and candidate entities in pairwise using the semantic relatedness between them. Then they use a random walk algorithm on the graph to solve the problem. However, they did not take the NIL problem into consideration. That is, in entity linking, if the referent entity of an name mention is not in our KB, it should be linked to a pseudo entity NIL. In our case, we should abandon the mapping of the current triple by deciding whether this entity has been listed in the KB(Zheng et al., 2010).

4.3 Knowledge base Propagation

Although we can extract millions of relations and built a KB in previous subsections, it has the same shortage as most existing KBs: the knowledge extracted are mostly statical attributes of entities (such as birthdate or occupation of a person) and can not describe the latest updates of an entity (such as a politician is currently visiting a country).

In order to settle this problem, we use the dynamical knowledge extracted from up-to-date data to expand our KB. One possible solution is extracting semantic event elements from online news. In this project, we will synchronies our KB with a Chinese newspaper, RenMinRiBao (People's Daily).

5 Current Work

Currently, we have extracted triples from the infoboxes of HudongBaike and built the base KB. Manual evaluation shows that the precision of structured content extraction is over 95%. Most errors are caused by the web page's own mistakes or editing errors in infoboxes.

To assess the quality of HudongBaike data, in our preliminary experiments(Yidong et al., 2012), we extract relation facts from plain HudongBaike articles without infoboxes in a way similar to Kylin. We focus on three categories, including 国家 (Nation), 人物 (Person) and 演员 (Actor or Actress). In each category we select several representative attributes from its infobox template. We manually annotated more than 200 testing examples for evaluation: 100 in Person, 33 in Nation and 91 in Actor or Actress. The results shows that the HudongBaike data can be used to extract knowledge facts with a high precision in all three categories: in 人物 the average precision is 79.43%, in 国家 it is 78.9%, and in 演员 it even goes up to 90.8%.

Distant Supervision We further adopt the approach of distant supervision(Mintz et al., 2009) in a Chinese dataset. We generate a dataset from RenMinRiBao with 10000 sentences, and each sentence contains at least a pair of entities which correspond to a knowledge triple in HudongBaike's infobox extraction. We use 60% of the sentences as training set and 40% as the testing set. Our experiments show that when the recall is 10%, we can obtain a high precision of 87%, which indicates the feasibility of our model. However, as the recall raises, the precision drops dramatically. For example, when the recall is 29% the precision is about 65%. This can be remedied by adopting more encyclopedia-specific filtering strategies and assumptions during the distant supervision modeling.

6 Conclusions

In this project, we proposed a framework to build KBs in Chinese. It uses the infoboxes of HudongBaike as a seed knowledge base, the articles of HudongBaike as extra textual resources, adopts the idea of distant supervision to extract knowledge facts from unstructured data and link the triples to build a knowledge base. This framework requires little manual work, and can be used in other reliable knowledge resources. Our preliminary experimental results are encouraging, showing that the HudongBaike provides reasonable resources for building knowledge bases and the distant supervision fashion can be adapted to work well in Chinese.

For the next, we will further adapt our framework into a self-training manner. By using higher threshold for confidence in distant supervision we can make sure the precision of extracted knowledge is high enough for bootstrapping. Then we put the extracted knowledge facts into the seed KB, and the framework will repeat iteratively. On the other hand, we can extract knowledge facts from other reliable knowledge resource, such as Wikipedia, academic literature, and merge knowledge from different resources into one KB. Moreover, we can also make our KB multilingual by adopting our framework in other languages.

References

Banko, M., Cafarella, M. J., Soderland, S., Broadhead, M., and Etzioni, O. (2007). Open information extraction from the web. In *Proceedings of IJCAI*, IJCAI'07, pages 2670–2676.

Bizer, C., Lehmann, J., Kobilarov, G., Auer, S., Becker, C., Cyganiak, R., and Hellmann, S. (2009). Dbpedia - a crystallization point for the web of data. *Web Semant.*, 7:154–165.

Etzioni, O., Cafarella, M., Downey, D., Kok, S., Popescu, A.-M., Shaked, T., Soderland, S., Weld, D. S., and Yates, A. (2004). Web-scale information extraction in knowitall. In *Proceedings of the 13th WWW*, WWW '04, pages 100–110.

Giles, J. (2005). Internet encyclopaedias go head to head. *Nature*, 438:900–901.

Han, X., Sun, L., and Zhao, J. (2011). Collective entity linking in web text: a graph-based method. In *SIGIR*, SIGIR '11, pages 765–774, New York, NY, USA. ACM.

Matuszek, C., Cabral, J., Witbrock, M., and DeOliveira, J. (2006). An introduction to the syntax and content of cyc. In *Proceedings of the 2006 AAAI Spring Symposium*.

Mintz, M., Bills, S., Snow, R., and Jurafsky, D. (2009). Distant supervision for relation extraction without labeled data. In *Proceedings of the Joint Conference of the 47th Annual Meeting of the ACL and the 4th IJCNLP of the AFNLP: Volume 2 - Volume 2*, ACL '09, pages 1003–1011.

Niles, I. and Pease, A. (2001). Towards a standard upper ontology. In *Proceedings of FIOS - Volume 2001*, pages 2–9. ACM Press, New York.

Riedel, S., Yao, L., and McCallum, A. (2010). Modeling relations and their mentions without labeled text. In *Machine Learning and Knowledge Discovery in Databases*, volume 6323 of *Lecture Notes in Computer Science*, pages 148–163. Springer Berlin / Heidelberg.

Stark, M. M. and Riesenfeld, R. F. (1998). Wordnet: An electronic lexical database. In *Proceedings of 11th Eurographics Workshop on Rendering*. MIT Press.

Suchanek, F. M., Kasneci, G., and Weikum, G. (2007). Yago: a core of semantic knowledge. In *Proceedings of WWW*, WWW '07, pages 697–706, New York, NY, USA. ACM.

Tim, B.-L., J., H., and O., L. (2001). The semantic web. *Scientific American*.

Wu, F. and Weld, D. S. (2007). Autonomously semantifying wikipedia. In *CIKM*, CIKM '07, pages 41–50, New York, NY, USA. ACM.

Wu, F. and Weld, D. S. (2008). Automatically refining the wikipedia infobox ontology. In *WWW*, WWW '08, pages 635–644, New York, NY, USA. ACM.

Yao, L., Riedel, S., and McCallum, A. (2010). Collective cross-document relation extraction without labelled data. In *Proceedings of EMNLP*, EMNLP '10, pages 1013–1023, Stroudsburg, PA, USA. Association for Computational Linguistics.

Yidong, C., Liwei, C., and Kun, X. (2012). Learning chinese entity attributes from online encyclopedia. In *Proceedings of IEKB workshop in APWeb 2012*.

Zheng, Z., Li, F., Huang, M., and Zhu, X. (2010). Learning to link entities with knowledge base. In *HLT-NAACL 2010*, pages 483–491, Stroudsburg, PA, USA.

Author Index